EDUCATION FOR PLANNING

Education
for Planning:
City,
State,
& Regional

BY HARVEY S. PERLOFF

Published for

Resources for the Future, Inc.

GREENWOOD PRESS, PUBLISHERS
WESTPORT, CONNECTICUT

Library of Congress Cataloging in Publication Data

Perloff, Harvey S
    Education for planning.

    Reprint of the 1957 ed. published by Johns Hop-
kins Press, Baltimore.
    Bibliography: p.
    Includes index.
    1. Cities and towns--Planning--Study and teach-
ing. 2. Regional planning--Study and teaching.
I. Title.
[NA9012.P4 1977]   711'.07'1173   77-23156
ISBN 0-8371-9474-1

Originally published in 1957 for Resources for the Future, Inc.,
by The Johns Hopkins Press, Baltimore

Reprinted with the permission of The Johns Hopkins University Press

Reprinted in 1977 by Greenwood Press, Inc.

Library of Congress catalog card number 77-23156

ISBN 0-8371-9474-1

Printed in the United States of America

PREFACE

The growth of formal planning activities by both public and private groups in the United States has been one of the concomitants of the rapid urbanization, the spread of industry, and the pressures on water, land, and energy resources in various regions of the country. Ours is a complex society and at points it is becoming a crowded society. Whether it is a matter of too many automobiles trying to get to the same area at the same time, or of too little water available for all the people moving into a particular region, we find that some things tend to get out of equilibrium unless rather careful provisions are made for the future.

This is strikingly evident at the urban-rural fringes of our cities, where urban subdivisions are spreading in crazy-quilt fashion across the countryside. Unless some order is brought into urban expansion, the costs of public services can become almost prohibitive, valuable farm land can needlessly be made unproductive, watersheds can be abused and water problems magnified, and open space for recreation can be pushed beyond the normal reach of most city folk. At the same time, at both ends of these fringe areas—within the heart of the city and out in the agricultural zones—other types of present and emerging environmental problems call for social foresight and planning.

In many governmental units—from city planning commissions and local soil conservation districts, through state planning-and-development agencies and departments of resources and of public works, and on up to federal bureaus—the techniques of planning are today increasingly needed and increasingly drawn upon. Persons with knowledge and skill in city and regional planning come more and more in demand in both public and private organizations. There are today serious shortages of trained personnel. The result is that many important planning tasks cannot be carried out and that others are handled, often ineptly, by inadequately trained persons.

The problems with which city and regional planning have to deal tend to be highly complex. It is no simple matter to plan for the redevelopment of the blighted sections of a city, or for the sensible location of a modern interurban highway system, or for the multiple-purpose development of a river basin. These are tasks that call for expertness, as well as for wisdom and a sense of democratic procedures. Poor planning can be worse than no planning at all.

How shall persons be trained for these demanding tasks? How shall knowledge necessary for city and regional planning be advanced? Some twenty-five colleges and universities have set up planning schools, mainly to train men and women for work in urban planning At the same time, schools of architecture, design, engineering, and law, social science departments, and different types of interdisciplinary committees at universities throughout the country provide a wide variety of individual courses and seminars on planning problems and techniques.

At many of the universities questions about the adequacy of existing planning education are being raised both by teachers of planning and by others, including university administrators. Questions are being asked about the appropriate relationship of planning education to various disciplines and fields of study— particularly engineering, architecture, the social sciences, and different specialist fields. There is much discussion about the various ways of organizing the training of planners. The problem of providing a sound educational background for persons who will be concerned with planning for natural resources development and conservation and other aspects of regional planning is increasingly being investigated by university committees and various groups of practitioners.

Both the planning profession and planning education seem to be at an important turning point. The situation would seem to be similar to that which existed in medical education at the turn of the century when experiments at the Johns Hopkins School of Medicine and other developments brought about an intensive review throughout the country of the problems of medical training. Today many persons, inside and outside the planning profession, have come to feel that we have entered a period in the United States when the question of sound education for work in city and regional planning is of immediate and widespread interest. An example of this is a bill recently introduced in the Senate which would provide, through fellowships, federal funds for planning education.

The three essays presented in this book are intended as a contribution to the discussion of planning education now under way. They raise the question of what is an appropriate intellectual, practical, and "philosophical" basis for the education of city and regional planners and attempt some tentative answers. They highlight certain guidelines which can be drawn from an examination of the main facets in the development of the fields of city and regional planning and of planning education—past, present, and future.

At this still early stage of planning education, one can hope to do little more than to probe analytically here and there, to bring together suggestive items from history, to draw upon one's own experience and that of others, to discuss the key issues involved with persons from many fields and representing different points of view. During the past year I have taken part in what has amounted to a seminar-by-correspondence. I have sent early drafts of my papers to many individuals: planners, resource experts, educators, social scientists, university administrators, and others. They have agreed and disagreed, they have pointed to weaknesses in my arguments, they have suggested new ideas, new arrangements. With no exceptions, the responses have been interested ones, and often presented with much valuable detail. Planning education is a subject about which people tend to hold strong views. I have learned much through this seminar-by-correspondence.

I want to express my gratitude to those who reviewed one or another of the three essays. I want particularly to thank those who have reviewed both the city planning and the regional planning essays or who read drafts of all three essays: Edward A.

Ackerman, Melville C. Branch, Marion Clawson, Henry Fagin, Carl Feiss, Richard L. Meier, Howard K. Menhinick, Dennis O'Harrow, Lloyd Rodwin, and William L. C. Wheaton. Valuable suggestions on general questions of education were provided by Benjamin Bloom, Irving Fox, Edward S. Mason, Ralph W. Tyler, Norman Wengert, and Gilbert F. White, and on special problems in education for planning by Tracy Augur, T. Ledyard Blakeman, Howard T. Fisher, Robert W. Hartley, Frank W. Herring, Walter Isard, Martin Meyerson, Harold V. Miller, Victor Roterus and his associates in the Office of Area Development, Roscoe C. Martin, and Coleman Woodbury. I am indebted to Joseph L. Fisher for his thorough and thoughtful review of the entire manuscript. Thanks are also due to Perry Norton for his encouragement and his valuable editorial assistance, and to Nadja Schocken for her intelligent handling of many drafts and endless revisions. My wife has been of major assistance in every phase of this undertaking.

The first essay was originally published in the *Journal of the American Institute of Planners,* in the Fall 1956 issue. The third essay was written in collaboration with John R. P. Friedmann.

Washington, D.C.   *Harvey S. Perloff*
May 1957

CONTENTS

EDUCATION FOR PLANNING

Education of

City Planners:

PART I / Past,

Present,

& Future

I Problems of Professional Education

City planning [1] in the United States has grown rapidly in scope, in complexity, and in the number of career opportunities the field provides. Almost every city in the United States, as well as many of the smaller urban communities, has established a planning agency or employs private planning consultants. In addition,

[1] The term "city planning" is used in its broadest sense, that is, referring to planning activities concerned with the entire urbanized area of broad metropolitan regions, as well as activities centering on small urban communities or the central city of a metropolis. "Urban planning," or "regional (metropolitan) planning" might be preferable terms as far as technical accuracy is concerned, but the term "city planning" has the advantage of wider understanding and traditional usage.

there are many redevelopment, housing, and urban renewal agencies and citizens' organizations employing trained planners. County and "regional" planning organizations, at times extending over very large areas, are being set up in every part of the country. An indication of the growth in planning activities is provided by the fact that the number of full-time employees of public planning agencies doubled in the decade after World War II, and membership in the major professional organizations more than doubled. At the same time many new opportunities for planners have opened up as consultants to, or employees of, private corporations undertaking various types of urban-development projects. Planners are being called upon to carry out activities of great variety and difficulty; activities which often directly influence the strength of the urban community's economic base and social fabric.

Looking ahead, it seems evident that with continued rapid urbanization, the increasing complexity of urban life, and an awakening sense among the American people of what our enormous national wealth and productivity can accomplish on the urban scene, still greater pressures for, and on, city planning can be expected.

In this context, the education of city planners in the United States is inadequate, both qualitatively and quantitatively.[2] The

2 As far as quantity is concerned, a gap between the demand for, and the supply of, trained planners has developed over the past decade and seems to be widening rather than closing. A survey of the personnel situation (mainly with regard to positions in public planning agencies) was provided by the Newsletter of the American Society of Planning Officials of February 1956 (Vol. 22, No. 2, pp. 9–10): "During 1954 we advertised just over 200 positions. During 1955 we advertised 413 positions. According to our records there are currently some 265 unfilled planning jobs. [Estimates of graduates from planning schools indicate that] Altogether, we can probably expect to add [a net total of] 170 planners in 1957, 180 in 1958, and perhaps 200 in 1959. . . . We would estimate that during 1956 there will be created 250 or more new jobs. We would also guess that if the supply of personnel were more adequate —if employers felt they had a better chance of getting someone—that number would be doubled. The rapidly expanding urban renewal program might double it anyway." It is, of course, difficult to prepare firm estimates of "supply" and "demand," since there is a good bit of variation in titles attached to positions concerned with different types of planning tasks, and since individuals with planning titles are sometimes involved in activities which have little if any relationship to the planning of urban communities.

planning educators themselves are the first to recognize this, and the first to welcome discussions of the problems of planning education. They know that they are not recruiting an adequate number of first-rate students into the university planning schools, that their curricula are not based on fundamentals and rely too heavily on bits and pieces of accumulated wisdom, that they are not contributing enough to the development of planning tools, and that their research—if there is any—is not sufficiently basic and must rely on research scholars trained in other fields.

Since the future of city planning is certain to be greatly affected by the type and quality of education provided in our institutions of higher learning, this is a significant problem for the entire planning profession and not alone for those directly associated with the planning schools. It is a problem also for the colleges and universities of the nation.

It is quite evident that many of the college and university administrators are confused about planning and education for planners. They are troubled by the controversies that seem to whirl continually about the planning school, by qualitative inadequacies, and by the fact that so many basic educational questions are as yet not even partially resolved. Is planning actually a separate field of study that needs a separate school, or is it an aspect of some other field like architecture or social science? Should it emphasize the design skills and an applied approach or should it provide a very broad training in a research-oriented environment? And so on. This disturbed feeling about planning education on the part of university administrators is no small matter. Their understanding and support is urgently needed if planning schools are to prosper—or even exist.

THE DEVELOPMENT OF PROFESSIONAL EDUCATION

Many of the problems of planning education are basically similar to those which plagued other professions at critical stages in their development.

In evaluating quantitative deficiencies, attention must be given to the fact that currently in the United States there is a general shortage of trained personnel in almost every field.

While each profession has its own special history and development, there are some important common elements which, if analogies are not carried too far, can be highly suggestive in analyzing the development of education in a particular profession. In some important respects planning education today is about where medical and legal education in the United States were at roughly the beginning of the century. In the case of medical education, this would be the period before the reforms instituted at the Johns Hopkins School of Medicine, and later the development of other great medical schools, led the way out of confusion and mediocrity. As Dr. Shryock points out in his review of medical education,

> Like the arts colleges, American medical schools had long been preoccupied simply with the transmission of learning; and most of them did even this in a superficial manner. . . . A commercial spirit permeated the profession. It is hard to realize, today, that it became easier to gain entrance to a medical school than to a good arts college; that the course in the former was much shorter than in the latter. . . . Medical research was pursued occasionally by only a few individuals. . . .[3]

It took a basic reorientation—which required a new kind of organization, new faculties, and new educational techniques—to bring medical education to a high level of excellence. It took the provision of professional training within a research-oriented environment, emphasis upon the advancement of knowledge rather than merely the transmission of knowledge, the appointment of full-time faculty members rather than part-time local practitioners, real clinical teaching, the limiting of admission to

[3] Richard H. Shryock, *The Unique Influence of the Johns Hopkins University on American Medicine* (Copenhagen: Ejnar Munksgaard, 1953), pp. 11–12. For some interesting parallels in the development of education for the legal profession, see Alfred Z. Reed, *Training for the Public Profession of the Law* (Boston: Updike-Merrymount, 1921); Sidney P. Simpson, *The New Curriculum of the Harvard Law School* (Cambridge: Harvard Law Review Association, 1938, reprinted from the *Harvard Law Review*, Vol. LI, No. 6); and Albert J. Harno, *Legal Education in the United States,* A Report Prepared for the Survey of the Legal Education, (San Francisco: Bancroft-Whitney, 1953). At the beginning of the century much of the legal education was characterized by the teaching of local and concrete law (as against national and generalized); a "dogmatic" use of textbooks (as against a critical examination of cases or original sources); in many cases, no entrance requirements for students; and a great deal of practitioner-teaching.

those who had completed college training (including training in the basic sciences), the lengthening of the course of studies, and the development of post-internship training in specialties. Also, it took the assumption of educational leadership by the full-time faculty members.

The amount and type of leadership in the guidance of professional education provided by the university scholars, as compared with the practitioners, may well be an excellent gauge of the maturity and progress of a professional group (even though practitioners have a special, and highly important, educational function to perform in every instance). In the case of city planning, it seems evident that the full-time planning faculty members are not yet providing the type of enlightened and vigorous leadership which is needed to bring education for the city planning profession to a high degree of excellence. But it is worth noting that the problem of leadership has been characteristic of all professions in the earlier stages of their development.

Usually professional education has been pushed into the universities by outside leaders of the profession, and the practitioners themselves have provided much of the instruction and have set the orientation of the training curriculum. Only some time later —in some cases, generations later—have the university scholars taken the reins and developed an educational program for the profession which reflects the ideals and resources of the universities, as well as the evolving—rather than the past and current— needs of the profession.

Some of the problems and difficulties of planning education, then, are those which are characteristic of an early stage in the development of education for almost any profession. In this connection we note that courses in city planning were not available in the United States until 1909 and that the first school of planning was established in 1929. Education for city planners is of relatively recent vintage.

Other types of problems and difficulties are quite specific to city planning, and therefore to planning education. Possibly outstanding among these is the confusion that has resulted from the fact that city planning in the United States has been influenced and guided by *two* relatively distinctive streams of development. These two streams have intertwined and in some sense even

merged, but each has enough of its own special elements to make
the process of merging an extremely difficult one.

"PROFESSIONAL" AND "ADMINISTRATIVE" ASPECTS

One stream of development in the city planning field has been
more or less typically professional in character; that is, *the evolution of a separate skill group* (a development similar to that in
the case of doctors, architects, and engineers)—here, a skill group
concerned with shaping and guiding the physical growth and
land-use arrangements of urban communities, through making
and applying plans and designs covering the location and three-
dimensional form of various types of public and private improvements upon the land. Central to this stream of development has
been the image of the individual, having met the requirements
of a professional society, serving a public or private client by
carrying out more or less clearly defined professional tasks. Over
time the tasks have been significantly broadened but, within this
line of development, the assumption has been that the individual
planner must himself learn and absorb the knowledge and skills
which the broadened tasks call for. This is a stream of development which began at the turn of the century with the city plans
produced by the architects and engineers turned city planners,
which was strengthened by the formation in 1917 of a professional association (the American City Planning Institute), and
which today sets the framework for some of the planning activities and much of the graduate planning education.

The other stream of development—which came to be a significant force in the 1930's and which has gained momentum since
then—has been *the evolution of an administrative function of
planning within municipal government.* This has been essentially
a staff advisory function, and increasingly a staff function which
organization-wise is similar to other staff (or central overhead)
functions such as budgeting and personnel management. The
planning function in local government has come to be concerned
with activities such as the programming (scheduling) of public
works and improvement projects, analysis of problems related to
the over-all economic and physical growth of the community,

and the making of recommendations as to means (legal controls, incentive payments, etc.) which might be employed to encourage private urban development and redevelopment activities. Central to this stream of development has been the emphasis on an administrative function carried out by an official planning agency, working within the political framework of the municipal government, concerned with certain aspects of all municipal activities (i.e., the over-all planning aspects) in the same way that the budgeting office is concerned with the allocation of funds to all municipal agencies or the central personnel office is concerned with civil service administration influencing all or most of the departments within the local government.

The focus in this stream of development has been on a function (rather than on a professional skill) and therefore the emphasis has been on a team effort and on the various skills that the team as a whole—and not any one individual member—must have. Just as the main focus in the other stream of development has been on plan making of a comprehensive sort, the focus in the latter stream has been on accomplishments in an administrative and political setting.

As suggested above, these two lines of development have crisscrossed, intertwined, and in some ways merged. Thus, the separate-skill-group development has involved a broadening conception of the professional skills required for city planning to include understanding and ability in the administrative-political realm. It has become quite widely accepted that the professional planner should have some training in administration and that he should seek to develop an understanding of politics as soon as he possibly can. On the other side, the administrative-political stream of development has involved the establishment of skill requirements in the recruitment of persons into official planning agencies which has ensured that most of those holding public planning posts have had training in the separate-skill-group tradition. This intertwining reflects the fact that city planning in the United States, in its public form, has been developing as a rather unique governmental function which joins together *general staff activities* (concerned with "integration" and balancing of municipal government operations, for example, through capital-improvement programming) and *substantive activities* concerned with guiding urban physical development (for example, through the preparation of master plans and the application of zoning and other controls to carry them out).

All this, however, is still in a relatively early stage of evolution and it is difficult to see all the implications. Thus, it is inevitable that discussions of city planning and of planning education should sometimes take the first (separate-skill-group) stream of development as the framework and stress what the "professional planner" has to know and be trained in; at other times, should refer to the administrative-political line of development and stress the team requirements; and still at other times (but, as yet, only rarely) should consider the implications of both lines of development and of the potentialities inherent in them.

A review of the main facets in the development of city planning is instructive in several ways. It serves to bring into focus the impact on the city planning field of a dual (instead of a uniform and consistent) line of development. Also, it is suggestive of the direction planning education should take if the latter is to turn the dual development into a source of strength rather than a cause of division and confusion.

II   *Development of the City Planning Field and of Planning Education*

City planning in the United States has gone through several stages, each of which has had its own special characteristics. The main features of the various stages are described in Appendix I–A, page 54, and landmarks in the history of city planning are briefly described there. During the sixty-some years since the beginning of the modern city planning movement in the United States (usually dated from the Chicago World's Fair of 1893), the functions of city planning and of the persons called planners have changed significantly. In an important sense, however, the most striking feature of the history of city planning has been what might be called its "cumulative" characteristics, the fact that the planning field has been broadened continuously as the scope for municipal government activities has grown and as various movements, ideas, professions, and studies have come to have an influence on city planning.[4]

Not unexpectedly, the course city planning took was quite directly related to the environmental context within which planning functioned—the social attitudes, the prevailing view of the appropriate scope for governmental activity, the types of groups that wielded economic and political power. And the training of planners, in turn, reflected the professional view of the kinds of skills needed by those carrying out planning activities.

THE EARLIER PHASE: ROLE OF THE ARCHITECT, LANDSCAPE ARCHITECT, AND ENGINEER

In this framework, it is instructive to examine the role of the architect, landscape architect, and engineer during the early period (the Chicago Fair of 1893 to World War I) precisely because this early history has profoundly influenced the entire development of city planning.

The latter part of the nineteenth century and the early part of the twentieth was a period in which the accepted scope for municipal activity was defined in limited terms and when extensive public control of private property was next to inconceivable. At

4 In this respect, the city planning profession in the United States has followed a course quite different from that of the town and country planning profession in Europe and elsewhere in the world. Outside of the United States, with some variations (as in Canada and Australia), the planning profession has in the main limited itself to physical planning and in very large part to the civic design aspects of such planning. For a brief description of the major characteristics of the planning profession and of planning education in the United States and abroad, see Frederick J. Adams, "The Status of Planning and Planning Education," *United Nations Bulletin on the Education of Planners* (mimeographed 1956). A description of programs provided by planning schools and an outline of the historical development of planning education in countries throughout the world is provided in the bulletin published by the International Federation for Housing and Town Planning, *Education in Town Planning: An International Survey* (The Hague, Netherlands, 1952).

the same time, however, many people were anxious to avoid the worst features of industrialization and urbanization: the ugliness, crowding, lack of public facilities. Also, there was a reaching out for status and symbols of achievement on the part of rich and powerful individuals and groups, particularly in the larger cities, through the creation of urban "monuments" such as civic centers, park systems, and broad thoroughfares—("I am a citizen of no mean city"). The civic improvement organization and the commerce club, sponsoring activities designed to improve the appearance and amenities of cities, grew up and flourished. Here was a context within which the "city beautiful" concept could be expected to emerge and within which the need for the planning of public improvements and park systems could become accepted and acceptable.[5] The architects and landscape architects could undertake the planning of civic centers, park systems, and thoroughfares as an extension of their established activities.

A similar logic appears in the further development of planning in the 1910's and 1920's. The increasing rapid urbanization, with its accompanying congestion and demands on public and private services and facilities, focused attention on problems of traffic and transportation, sanitation, and a wide range of public improvements. Add, further, the high value placed on the efficient functioning of cities by a controlling business community that had come to think of efficiency in government as "good business," and one can understand why the "city practical" concept should have developed and why there should have been a receptivity for the ideas and skills of the engineers as well as of the architects. These professionals were the experts in construction and efficient functioning; it is hardly surprising that they should have come to the forefront in an Age of Building.

It is a matter of no small importance that many members of these professions were men of skill, imagination, and vision. The new planning activities were not foisted upon them. Certainly, their skills fitted them for the key planning tasks *as then seen,* but they themselves were the ones who developed city planning

5 Although the drive for civic improvement was strong enough to get a great number of plans on paper, it was not strong enough to get very many projects built.

as a new professional field and who laid the foundations at each
stage for a continually broadening view of planning and what it
should attempt to achieve. Thus, even in the earliest period, some
of the plans demonstrated the inherent logic of public control of
certain private activities, as in connection with transportation
and traffic, and the need for the extension of the common law of
nuisances. Daniel H. Burnham could say as early as 1909, in his
Plan of Chicago, "It is no attack on private property to argue that
society has the inherent right to protect itself against abuses."

Until the end of the 1920's education for city planning as such
was quite limited. Most training took place on an apprenticeship
basis in the offices of planning practitioners. The first formal university training in city planning was not introduced until 1909,
and then only as a few separate courses given to students of landscape architecture. Training in architecture, landscape architecture, and engineering was then seen as adequate for the planning
tasks. Not until 1923 was city planning accepted as a graduate
specialization, and then only in one department in one university
(Harvard).

The establishment of a separate school of planning (at Harvard
University) in 1929 marked, after a full generation of planning
activity, the recognition, at least on the part of some practitioners
and educators, of the need for separate teaching facilities for city
planning.

LAYING THE FOUNDATION FOR A BROAD VIEW OF PLANNING

One cannot examine the Chicago Plan of 1909, or read the
papers given at the early national planning conferences or the
early zoning reports, without being struck by the breadth of conception and the far-reaching vision of many of the planners of
the period.[6] Thus, almost from the very start, the stage was set
for the constantly widening view of the planning field which has
taken place since then. Over the years there came in fairly quick
succession a whole set of *additions* to the conception as well as the

[6] John M. Gaus, *The Education of Planners* (Cambridge: Harvard University, Graduate School of Design, 1943), pp. 7–10.

practice of planning. From (1) an early stress on planning as concerned chiefly with esthetics, planning came to be conceived also in terms of (2) the efficient functioning of the city—in both the engineering and the economic sense; then (3) as a means of controlling the uses of land as a technique for developing a sound land-use pattern; then (4) as a key element in efficient governmental procedures; later (5) as involving welfare considerations and stressing the human element; and, more recently, (6) planning has come to be viewed as encompassing many socio-economic and political, as well as physical, elements that help to guide the functioning and development of the urban community. Similarly, from a tendency to focus on the isolated project (the civic center, the lake front), the point of view and, to some degree at least, the function of planning has been enlarged to encompass the whole city, then the larger metropolitan community, and, here and there, there has been demonstrated an awareness of the intimate and vital relationship of the city to other cities, and to the region, the state, and the nation.

It is certainly true that much of this broadening has not been really absorbed as yet, that it is often quite superficial, that there is a continuous falling back on the narrower, purely physical and isolated-project point of view. But it is at least equally true that the slipping back tends to become less and less frequent and not quite as far back, as times goes on. It is important to stress this point as background for the view, which I will develop later, that the planning schools need not be nearly as cautious and apologetic as they have been about broadening their planning curricula. This would, in fact, only parallel the actual development of the planning field, and not be the startling innovation that some planning educators seem to think.

ROLE OF THE LAWYER AND THE SOCIAL SCIENTIST

The lawyers were the first professional group, outside of the architects, landscape architects, and engineers, to take a significant part in city planning, both practically and "conceptually." By the time of the first World War, a number of lawyers were already devoting their main attention to city planning, and several lawyers were among the small group of professional planners to form the American City Planning Institute in 1917.

Practicing lawyers, as well as legal scholars and the courts, laid the foundations for what were to become the major legal tools associated with city planning—zoning and subdivision control—through the development of legal concepts centering on the police power and eminent domain.[7] They also figured prominently in the erection of a legal framework for city planning in the United States through the statutes of the individual municipalities (mainly zoning ordinances) and through state enabling legislation, particularly the extremely important "model" enabling legislation for city planning and zoning promulgated by advisory committees of the U.S. Department of Commerce in the 1920's. A small but highly influential group of lawyers—men like Edward Bassett and Alfred Bettman—also served actively on planning commissions and on special study groups, and in other ways played an important role in city planning.

The history of the development of zoning and other legal tools which came to be so closely associated with city planning illustrates rather well the flexible manner in which city planning in the United States drew on, enriched, and gave direction to a variety of movements and conceptions relating to urban development (provided that these were in tune with the times, i.e., provided they fitted into the prevailing socio-economic-political environment). Zoning could, of course, be accepted as a tool not only of orderly urban growth but for the preservation and increase of property values—undoubtedly a crucial factor in its relatively early adoption.

The social "environment" element perhaps also played a significant part in the rather late incorporation into city planning of the approaches, techniques, and personnel from the social sciences. The social scientists began to probe into urban questions at a fairly early stage. By the time of World War I, Professor Ely and his colleagues and students at the University of Wis-

---

7 Edward M. Bassett, *Zoning* (New York: Russell Sage Foundation, 1936); Alfred Bettman, *City and Regional Planning Papers*, City Planning Studies No. 13, (Cambridge: Harvard University Press, 1946).

consin were already deep into the problems of land economics, including urban land economics. Ely's monumental treatise on *Property and Contract* was published in 1914.[8] By 1925, Ely's Research Institute could sponsor a journal devoted to problems of land and public utility economics. In the 1920's also, significant advances in the study of the urban community were made through the research of social scientists at the University of Chicago, men such as R. E. Park and E. W. Burgess in Sociology, Charles C. Colby in Geography, and Charles E. Merriam in Political Science.[9] At other universities as well the social scientists were making available a body of detailed knowledge about the city and developing insights and techniques of great potential value for city planning.

But the social scientists who were concerned with urban questions tended to emphasize disturbing social and economic problems—such as slums and inadequate housing, social disorganization in the urban communities, and inadequate public services and facilities, speculation and abuse of land—matters which in the 1910's and 1920's were as yet generally deemed to be largely outside the scope of legitimate municipal government activities (although some municipal reform legislation, e.g., with regard to tenements, were already on the statute books). As Robert Walker suggests:

> The leaders of the planning movement made an invaluable contribution to good government and to the acceptance of the planning idea between 1920 and 1930. Consultants, members of planning commissions, and civic leaders in private organizations argued the need for planning in city government on countless occasions, gradually arousing public interest and bringing about the creation of official planning agencies in practically all the important cities of the country. On the other hand, the sources of the strongest support for planning [in the 1920's] were not those from which one would anticipate serious agita-

8 Richard T. Ely, *Property and Contract in their Relation to the Distribution of Wealth* (New York: The Macmillan Co., 1914); also Richard T. Ely and Edward W. Morehouse, *Elements of Land Economics* (New York: The Macmillan Co., 1924) and Richard T. Ely and George S. Wehrwein, *Land Economics* (Ann Arbor: Edwards Brothers, 1938).

9 For a review of the work of the Chicago social scientists during the 1920's, see T. V. Smith and Leonard D. White, eds., *Chicago: An Experiment in Social Science Research* (Chicago: University of Chicago Press, 1929).

tion for a frontal attack upon slums, poverty, disease, and other municipal problems then being glossed over by urban governments.[10]

It was not until the depression of the 1930's had altered both social attitudes and the accepted fields of municipal government activity that city planning quite seriously began to draw on the social sciences.[11] In the depression years, the planning agencies expanded their efforts to encompass a much wider field than public works and zoning. The planning commissions, responding to the stimulus of available federal funds, entered energetically into planning for slum clearance and housing. Incidental to the preparation of applications for housing projects, they collected data on such phases of city life and government as crime, disease, income, industry, the cost of rendering municipal services, and tax delinquency. Increasingly, social science materials and methods and social scientists came to play a significant role in city planning.

ADMINISTRATION TO THE FOREFRONT

The depression not only focused attention on social problems, but also highlighted questions of administration and organization.[12] Interest in efficient government and in "management" had at an early stage come to have some influence on city planning, but it was not until official public planning agencies had

10 Robert A. Walker, *The Planning Function in Urban Government* (Chicago: University of Chicago Press, revised edition, 1950), p. 35.

11 A notable exception was the *Regional Plan of New York and Its Environs*, which was prepared under the direction of a committee organized in 1922 and which was published in 1929. The plan comprised a series of survey volumes which dealt with problems of population, industry and economic development, land values, government, public services and facilities, and metropolitan growth and arrangement, which made substantial use of social science knowledge and techniques. The Regional Plan, however, stood alone in the city planning field in this respect. Together with the establishment of the first planning school, the Regional Plan symbolized the transition from the earlier historical phase in city planning to the "modern" phase.

12 An extremely useful discussion of the problems of planning organization and administration is provided in Walker, *op. cit.*, particularly chapters IV–VII.

undertaken the city planning function and displaced the private civic organizations, and not until the study of public administration had gained some stature, that questions of administration and governmental organization in city planning received active and detailed consideration. Thus, for example, the Urbanism Committee of the National Resources Committee was composed chiefly of administrators and students of administration. Their famous report, *Our Cities: Their Role in the National Economy* (1937), as well as their supplementary report, *Urban Government* (1939), seriously probed the problems of planning organization and administration. Also, over time, an increasing number of university-trained public administrators joined staffs of city planning agencies. They brought with them definite ideas about the need for integrating the planning agency more closely with the structure of local government.

But it was, undoubtedly, the force of circumstances which brought to city planning what amounted to a new line of development, a new dimension. Municipal officials, as well as students of public administration, came increasingly to see that the city planning agency could perform many quite practical administrative tasks which would help to solve pressing problems, especially when there is much to do and few funds to do it with. The preparation of informational reports of all sorts, capital-improvement programming, and capital budgeting came to be ongoing activities of many of the municipal planning agencies. This movement toward planning as a staff activity gathered so much momentum after World War II, in fact, that questions have been raised as to whether the main purposes of urban planning were not being lost in the pressure of short-term administrative activities.

THE 1940's AND 1950's

World War II and the postwar era accentuated the changing orientation of planning which came into being during the depression. The planning of housing for war workers and the preparation during the war of a "shelf" of local public works plans in the event of a postwar depression focused attention on the economic and social elements of planning. This was true also of the rapid population and industrial changes which took place during World War II and which continued in force in the postwar period. One consequence was to make more clear to local communities that useful physical planning can proceed only on the basis of adequate information about the economic and industrial foundation upon which they rest. Thus, a number of city planning commissions undertook studies of the economic base of their communities.

During the past decade—in part at least, as a consequence of the federal aid made available for public housing, urban redevelopment, and urban renewal—city planning has become increasingly concerned with the social and economic aspects, as well as the physical aspects, not only of housing and slum clearance, but of many features of the urban scene. A new appreciation has been developing of the human elements in city development and city planning.[13] Also, attention has been turned to the problems of making large-scale planned developments attractive to private capital, particularly in connection with redevelopment and renewal projects. At the same time many new opportunities for planners have opened up as consultants to, or employees of, private corporations undertaking various types of urban-development projects, including the construction of entire new cities on open land.

Looking back over the history of city planning, it becomes

13 Walter H. Blucher, former executive director of the American Society of Planning Officials, aptly characterized the changing approach to city planning in the following terms: "In the early part of this century, the emphasis in city planning was on the city beautiful. During the twenties, it was on the city practical. Today, the emphasis is on the human beings who populate a community. The city is intended to serve humans; humans are not intended to serve the city (although they do have a duty and a responsibility to the city as a governmental unit). With these changes in attitudes, could the theory and practice in planning have stood still?" "Has the Technique of Planning Changed?" *Newsletter, American Society of Planning Officials* (April 1949), p. 33. In his editorials in the ASPO *Newsletter*, Walter Blucher for many years provided a lively current record of events, ideas, and controversies in the city planning field, and himself provided many valuable suggestions. Dennis O'Harrow, as the new executive director of ASPO, is continuing this valuable record of developments in city planning, and adding his own views of the current scene.

clear that both the term "planning" and city planning activities
have served extremely useful social ends. Planning—as an approach, a symbol, and an activity—has helped to bring to the
forefront, and into the consciousness of governments and of the
general public, the importance and desirability of being concerned (operationally) with relationships among people, physical
objects, and ecological forces; of trying to see things whole; of
setting goals and of trying to figure out the best ways of achieving
them; of trying to co-ordinate and integrate the different kinds
of physical improvement and development activities carried out
by the government; of aiming at and working toward a better
future. Thus, at least in the United States, a dynamic relationship
has developed between city planning as an idea and an activity,
on the one side, and, on the other, the broadening popular view
of municipal government responsibility and the more widespread
acceptance of the need for consciously working toward an improved urban environment.

HOW THE EDUCATION OF CITY PLANNERS HAS EVOLVED

The various phases in the education of city planners followed
quite closely the development of the city planning field itself.
This can be seen by relating the educational background of
planners to the different phases in the history of city planning.

As noted above, city planning in the United States has developed through a series of additions and extensions, continually
absorbing new techniques and adding new tasks. This "absorp-
tive" quality has been true of planning education as well. At
most planning schools, three-dimensional design and site and
project planning from the beginning were the central elements
in the training of planners. Most of the teaching and most of the
student work centered about the drafting board.[14] Somewhere

14 It is not surprising, considering the long period during which the physical and design aspects of city planning were predominant, that the earlier city
planning curricula should have centered on design and project planning and
that "professionalization" should have jelled more or less around this phase
of city planning. Yet 1929 saw the first planning school established. This was
also the year when the *Regional Plan of New York and Its Environs* was published, with its sophisticated use of social science materials and techniques and

along the line, social science subjects were introduced into the planning curriculum—e.g., some land economics—and social science students began to take degrees in planning.[15] Later, the regional aspects of urban planning began to be considered. And later still (at a few schools) some serious research work was undertaken and planning students were encouraged to do research themselves. Five of the twenty-two planning schools which were in existence in 1954—when Frederick Adams published his survey of planning education—(all of them started in the 1940's) were organized through the stimulation of social science departments and tended to put at least some emphasis on the social sciences. These schools have also led the way in organizing research programs in problems of urbanism and planning.

The over-all educational picture is, then, one of gradual assimilation of social science, regional aspects, and research into planning curricula—but always with a considerable lag. In general, it has only been long after the practitioners found themselves ill equipped to undertake tasks thrust upon them—tasks such as population and migration analyses, regional economic surveys, and the development of programming and capital-budgeting techniques—that the universities responded with changes in their existing training programs or initiated new planning programs. On the whole, planning education has tended to follow somewhat haltingly after the march of practical events, rather than to anticipate needs and to develop new knowledge and methods. Also it should be noted that in only two or three planning schools has the "assimilation" process gone very far to date. Most of the planning schools have as yet gone very little beyond urging students to take some courses in the social sciences or to

with its broad conceptions of both the planning tasks and the area over which urban planning should extend. It wasn't until the 1940's that university planning education really caught up with the Regional Plan of New York.

[15] The entry of social science students into planning has been gaining momentum. Frederick J. Adams reports, in his *Urban Planning Education in the United States* (Cincinnati: Alfred Bettman Foundation, 1954, p. 15), that in the school year 1951–52, in the nineteen schools with graduate programs, 34.5 per cent of the students registered received their undergraduate training in one of the social sciences. (38 per cent of the students were from architecture or landscape architecture, 11 per cent from engineering, and 16.5 per cent from other fields, including the humanities.)

refer in lectures to the importance of looking at regional factors in urban planning.

The training of city planners at the universities has until quite

TABLE 1   *Stages in the Education of City Planners*

Historical phase	Educational background of city planners
Earlier Phase: 1893 (Chicago World's Fair) *to World War I* Main focus on "City Beautiful."	ARCHITECTURE OR LANDSCAPE ARCHITECTURE
Earlier Phase: World War I to late 1920's Main emphasis on public-works and land-use planning (the "City Practical").	ARCHITECTURE LANDSCAPE ARCHITECTURE CIVIL ENGINEERING LAW (in a few cases) A few planning practitioners with one or more courses in planning (taken in schools of architecture and landscape architecture).
Modern Phase: 1928–29 to 1939 Greater attention to social problems; city planning increasingly becoming an administrative (overhead staff) function in municipal government. Planning schools established at Harvard (1929), MIT (1935), Cornell (1935), and Columbia (1937).	ARCHITECTURE LANDSCAPE ARCHITECTURE CIVIL ENGINEERING LAW OR SOCIAL SCIENCE CITY PLANNING (as such)—very few Many planning practitioners with some courses in Planning; a few with degrees in Planning.
Modern Phase: 1940 to present Increase in scope and areal extent of planning activities; importance of federal aid, particularly in urban redevelopment and renewal; 18 planning schools established between 1941 and 1954.	PLANNING ARCHITECTURE LANDSCAPE ARCHITECTURE CIVIL ENGINEERING LAW OR SOCIAL SCIENCE Most planning practitioners with some training in Planning; many with degrees in Planning.*

* In October 1952, there were 538 alumni of planning schools, 431 of whom had graduate degrees in planning. A much larger number, of course, had taken courses in planning schools. Frederick J. Adams, *Urban Planning Education in the United States* (Cincinnati: Alfred Bettman Foundation, 1954), p. 17.

recently been mainly in the hands of planning practitioners—men who devoted much of their time to private practice while they were teaching, or who considered themselves to be *transmitting* to students the knowledge they had acquired in long years of practice. Until the last decade or so, planning education, thus, has been essentially an extension of the field of planning practice. Teaching by practitioners had special import stemming from the fact that these men had, with few exceptions, been trained in architecture, landscape architecture, or engineering. There was a strong tendency to depend on familiar tools and approaches (such as heavy reliance on the drafting board) merely because they were familiar and not because careful evaluation had shown them to be effective as educational techniques in city planning training. Also, in an earlier period the technical requirements of the planner were rather rudimentary and, at the same time, the individual planning-consultant led a somewhat tenuous existence, so that it was not surprising that the practitioner glided back and forth between planning and his "mother trade."

Since World War II, as city planning became more firmly established as a separate profession, and a graduate planning degree became increasingly a requirement for both public and private planning positions, the planning schools have begun to rely more heavily on full-time faculty members. In some cases, however, the qualitative gains have been questionable. A full-time teacher who falls back on the transmission of bits and pieces of "practical wisdom" is likely to be less effective and useful than an able part-time practitioner-teacher who can bring his students into intimate contact with practical work in the field.

The important criterion—in planning education, as in other professional education—is, of course, whether the faculty members are individuals whose careers are devoted to expanding the knowledge, principles, and methods of the field, rather than merely to transmitting knowledge and methods already widely employed.

The history of city planning serves to underline very sharply why planning education cannot rely on the transmission of existing knowledge and methods in a traditional "apprenticeship" manner, but must be geared to the continuing search for new knowledge and methods and the development of a basic "core" curriculum at the heart of planning education. As indicated above, the very functions of city planning have been changing at breath-taking speed, with major changes taking place not in a matter of generations, but in a matter of a few years. The students being trained today must be prepared for many such changes during their working lifetime.

Also, an examination of the history of city planning highlights the extent to which planning has evolved by drawing on the knowledge, methods, and personnel from a large number of professions and academic disciplines. Appendix I–B (page 62) outlines some of the intellectual and professional contributions to, and influences on, city planning. Even a bare outline of these contributions and influences suggests the richness of the sources from which city planning has drawn or is now beginning to draw. But the very breadth of the actual and potential intellectual and professional contributions makes it evident that a sound planning education cannot be pieced together by drawing on a little bit here and a little bit there. Only if planning students are required to have a rounded general education as a prerequisite for graduate training, and if the training of city planners centers about a carefully designed core curriculum, can this surrounding richness be a source of strength for city planning education rather than a source of confusion and dilution.

III   *Some Trends and Their Implications for Planning*

The main concern of city planning and of planning education must, obviously, be with the evolving situation and with the near and longer-run future. Special attention might well be paid to the trends that are likely to have a far-reaching and profound influence on planning. It is not a question so much of "looking into the future" as it is a question of not overlooking fairly well-established trends and developments already on the horizon.

A GREAT AGE OF URBAN BUILDING AND REBUILDING

A trend certain to have a profound influence on city planning and city planners is the impressive continuing increase in our national wealth and income—that 3 per cent compounded, annual rise in gross national product. This increase, joined with scientific and technological progress, suggests a future of greater opportunities for better family and community living.[16]

We look forward to more family income and leisure. Projecting what is happening now, we can see that city planning is likely to be influenced by the changing attitudes and activities of urbanites, including:

a greater sensitivity to the environment of family activities;
greater participation in, and use of, cultural activities and facilities;
ever-increasing demand for recreational facilities;
greater demands made on public services and facilities, including greater use of the highways by multi-car families;
insistence on a wide choice of alternatives in community environment and living patterns, so that satisfactory living can be achieved at every stage of the life cycle.

It may well be that the American people are only now beginning to sense what our great national wealth and productivity can accomplish on the urban scene. Some important lessons are being learned: for example, that a public-private partnership (as in urban redevelopment) can be remarkably effective in getting things done and that more can be accomplished through positive developmental planning than through negative controls.

What are the implications for planning? One of the most important is the likelihood that there will be more and more individual "urban development" projects—new subdivisions and new towns (the Levittowns and Park Forests of the past decade are in all likelihood only the beginning), many slum-clearance and redevelopment projects, many neighborhood "renewal" projects, and similar individual developments. And these will have to be

16 Assuming that we have the wit and good luck to avoid both serious depression and war.

.

planned as separate projects (even if in a larger context), in detail and in three-dimensional terms. Some of these are being, and will continue to be, planned by public agencies, but many are likely to be planned by private consultant firms. What kind of planners will these private consultants be? Will they have a sense of public responsibility? Will they be individuals of depth, or narrow technicians? Imaginative, creative solutions to the problems of modern urban living will be at a premium. Will planners in both the private and the public realms be among the foremost groups in providing such solutions? Will "private" and "public" planners have a common base of training and a common language so that they can achieve an effective type of public-private co-operation? Here is a great challenge for the U.S. planning schools.

The other side of the coin may well be that the very number of individual projects being carried out will highlight the importance of comprehensive planning on a region-wide basis as never before. It may well be that we can look forward to an ever-increasing appreciation of the need for planning for orderly urban development, with very lively—meaning, politically conscious—concern on the part of urbanites as to just what is being planned for and against.

MORE FEDERAL ACTIVITY IN THE URBAN FIELD

Another trend worth noting is the increasingly important role of the federal government in urban planning and development. Both the scope and size of federal contributions to urban communities have been increasing. Federal aid for roads, certain types of waterworks, hospitals, housing, and slum clearance have been important in metropolitan development for some time, while financial assistance for redevelopment and urban renewal as well as for community planning, metropolitan studies, and "demonstration projects" are highly significant postwar phenomena.

The trend suggests that federal aid to urban communities can be expected to increase significantly, particularly considering the superior fiscal capacity of the federal government. Substantial federal assistance for the construction of schools is on the horizon. There is a strong likelihood that the federal helping hand will be extended to other "public works" as time goes on. It isn't too hard to imagine that once the variety of national grants to cities proliferates, the aid may be packaged into a general federal grant for "urban public facilities."

The increase in federal financial assistance to cities can be expected to be accompanied by stricter and more seriously enforced federal provisions as to the type and quality of community planning that must be under way before a city can qualify for federal aid. National aid to assist communities in their planning is already established, and grants for this purpose are likely to increase in amount and scope. It does not seem too far-fetched to assume that in the not too distant future the federal government may establish a department of urban affairs and support the states in establishing "urban extension services." Through such services, the most advanced technical know-how might be brought to cities by specially trained personnel—"urban extension agents." [17]

With the overwhelming majority of the American people living in urban communities (for example, it is entirely possible that by 1975 the urban population may be some 70 per cent or more of the total population of the country), there seems a very strong likelihood that urban problems will increasingly be of direct national concern and increasingly be conceived in national terms. How far away are we from the time when national politics will be largely urban politics, when the major parties will be concerned mainly with vying for the city vote? How long will it be before the national government openly recognizes metropolitan resources as among the most important resources of the nation?

What are the implications of this? Certainly, one can expect more and more attention to be given to the city-region (i.e., the entire area of urban "dominance") as the focus of urban and

[17] Such a service, or federal aid in general, would in no way replace the need for fiscal reform which would permit municipalities to obtain a more adequate share of public revenues. Cities must be in a position where they can do most things for themselves; federal aid and special services should be no more than useful supplements.

regional studies and ultimately of urban and regional planning.[18] Can the federal government long continue to act as though the local neighborhood was its natural focus of interest? For the moment this is the most readily accepted approach, but once federal interest in the urban field becomes more firmly established, the federal government is likely to turn its attention to the matters that are more directly of national interest—e.g., urban-agricultural relations at the urban fringe and the whole problem of metropolitan structure, industrial location and movement of materials and products, the urban communications and transportation network, the optimum use of public utilities, and so on. One can expect large numbers of persons to be concerned with these questions both within the federal government and within the urban communities.

GROWTH OF DEPARTMENTAL AND
OTHER AGENCY PLANNING

More and more persons carrying out planning tasks are employed by municipal agencies other than a planning commission. Not only is an ever-increasing amount of planning done by housing, redevelopment, and urban renewal agencies, but many planning activities of an important nature are carried out by planning units within city boards of education, departments of public works, departments of health and sanitation, and so on. This is certainly all to the good, since it would be unfortunate if departmental functions of the municipal government were carried out without attention to the orderly development of capital improvements and without programming of major departmental activities, or if redevelopment and renewal programs were carried out without careful attention to project land uses, project design, etc. But this raises some important questions.

How well equipped are the present city plan commissions and their employees to bring the many separate departmental plans and programs into meaningful over-all plans and programs? Are

18 See the suggestive article by John R. P. Friedmann, "The Concept of a Planning Region," *Land Economics*, Vol. 32 (February 1956), pp. 1–13.

planners in the central planning office carrying out what is supposed to be one of their key jobs—that of assisting in the executive task of co-ordination and integration—or are they actually far removed from the planning as well as the operations of the various municipal agencies?

The requirements are easy to state. The planners within the city plan commission should be fully aware that the work of their agency is only a part of the whole planning function of the city government; that one of their most important jobs is that of helping the municipal officials to evolve a framework for departmental and other planning (long term objectives, strategy, standards) and to help in co-ordinating and integrating the many separate planning activities of the government—that is, bringing the plans of the individual operating departments into "harmonious adjustment." Ideally, the city plan commission should have both the interest and talent to strengthen the planning role of the operating departments; to encourage, stimulate, and guide departmental planning. Also, both the planners within the central agency and the departmental planners should understand each others' problems, approaches, and techniques. If all the planners involved in the specialized tasks of the individual departments have no understanding and little interest in the central tasks of the city planning commission, then the job of integration becomes next to impossible.

Here is a real challenge for the planning schools. In the first instance, they must attract to their courses the individuals who are likely to do the departmental planning—the public health officer who is interested in administration, the engineer who is interested in highway planning, and similar individuals—so that they take training in planning as well as in their fields of specialization. And at least equally important is the need to provide a common core of training so that both the persons who will be the "central" planners and those who will be the departmental planners and the planning specialist-consultants will have had a significant common experience and will tend to speak the same language. The latter is particularly important since in actual practice, planners tend to move about rather freely from one type of planning position to another.

PLANNING AS A STAFF ACTIVITY

One of the most important of the trends worth noting is the changing form and function of municipal planning activity.

City planning has been getting away from the earlier approach —which involved a semi-independent "nonpartisan" planning commission, set up in a vague advisory capacity, concerned mainly with sponsoring a long-time, mapped, physical master plan as drawn up by a consultant, and with preparing and executing detailed zoning and subdivision regulations. Serious criticism was levied against this approach, and justifiably; this type of planning was removed from the people and lacked democratic support; it was outside the main stream of political action and municipal administration; it was essentially static and could not keep up with the rapid pace of urban development. The campaign to bring planning into the center of things has, in many instances, been largely accomplished. The public planning agency is becoming a more integral part of the municipal government machinery, and is likely to become even more so in the future.[19]

Desirable as this development may be, it brings in its train a number of serious problems. Thus, for example, direct contact with the current political problems of the city government has had a significant impact on the work programs of the planning agency. The load of day-by-day routines and crises has steadily increased, thus reducing time available to the staff for long-range planning studies and for the design of alternative solutions for the basic urban problems. With the additional administrative and "political" duties, planning agencies have found it necessary to contract with consulting firms for more and more of the basic planning studies as well as for specific project design. Professor Goodman, in an article analyzing the current functions of official planning agencies, estimates that today "only about 30 per cent of the effort of typical planning agencies is spent on matters that

---

[19] That this is a normal enough development has been stressed by Robert A. Walker (*op. cit.*, p. 134). He points out that practically all existing municipal functions—including police, fire, public works, health, and welfare services—have gone through a period of being administered by an independent board and have only gradually been assimilated into the administrative hierarchy of city government.

are removed from day-to-day referrals or services. The remaining 70 per cent is absorbed in short-term operations." [20]

It is not enough merely to point out that the city planning agency should be a staff arm of the chief executive—this is already clearly the organizational direction of city planning; the *kind* of staff work to be done and the manner in which it is to be done are the issues for the future. And these issues are, of course, of direct significance for planning education, since what is involved here is the question of what the planner in a public planning agency is going to be doing on the job, and the type of training he will need.

It seems to me that on the whole too much emphasis has been placed on the appropriate organizational place for public planning activities and that not nearly enough attention has been given to the questions of what is a sensible *administrative approach* to public planning and what is the appropriate *content* of such planning. In terms of political-administrative arrangements and in terms of the content of planning activities, there are sound aspects to the older approach to planning as well as unfortunate and fruitless features. On the other side, the newer approach opens up the highly undesirable possibility of a short-sighted, day-to-day patchwork of activities. If city planning is to be truly effective, it will be necessary to work out organizational arrangements and administrative techniques that will tend to retain the best features of the more traditional approach while shifting public planning activities to a sound staff basis.

By overstating differences somewhat, the major features of both the more traditional approach (involving a semi-independent agency concentrating on a long-term master plan) and of the newer approach (involving the planning agency as a staff arm of the executive) [21] can be shown to have both an "undesirable" and a "desirable" form.

20 William I. Goodman, "The Future of Staff Planning," *Journal of the American Institute of Planners*, Vol. 22 (Winter 1956), p. 27.

21 A forceful case for this general approach is presented by Charles S. Ascher, "City Planning, Administration—and Politics," *Land Economics*, Vol. 30 (November 1954), pp. 320–28. The best known case for an independent position for the municipal planning agency has been presented by Rexford G. Tugwell, "The Fourth Power," *Planning and Civic Comment*, Vol. 5 (April-June 1939).

TABLE 2   *Some Good and Bad Features of Two Approaches to City Planning*

"Undesirable" form	*"Desirable" form*

I. THE APPROACH INVOLVING A SEMI-INDE-
PENDENT PLANNING COMMISSION CONCERNED
MAINLY WITH A LONG-RANGE MASTER PLAN

	The Master Plan, periodically revised, seen as focusing attention on the longer-term problems and the longer-term development of the community; setting up generalized goals, a general strategy of development, and broad standards for the day-by-day activities. The plan accepted officially by the legislature at each major revision.
The Master Plan: viewed mainly as a series of maps and drawings, presenting a static (more or less once-for-all) view of the future of the city. Inflexible and basically inapplicable.	
Emphasis in the planning on the Grand Design, with a concentration on dominant physical features—the thoroughfares, park system, and the public facilities, and on specific land-use designations for every part of the city. Little, if any attention to the dynamic and continually changing forces that determine urban development.	*Emphasis* on (1) the strategic features in urban development, such as the "activity" centers (industrial, commercial, recreational) and the highway system (consciously setting a sensible pattern for urban expansion); on (2) standards for individual development projects (both public and private); and on (3) fitting departmental programs into a coherent pattern.
Independence of the planning commission achieved through its organizational position and, in general, its removal from the main stream of politics and municipal administration—and for that reason, the planning largely ineffectual and unused. Stress on the independence feature.	The basic approach at its most sensible suggests a view of planning as concerned with the more basic and longer-range questions rather than the more immediate matters having temporary political import; also suggests the desirability of placing a high value on the contributions of the expert and the creative planner —within a democratic and responsible framework.

"Undesirable" form	"Desirable" form

II. THE APPROACH INVOLVING AN OFFICIAL
PLANNING AGENCY SERVING AS A STAFF ARM
OF THE CHIEF EXECUTIVE

Closeness to politics forcing the planning agency to work on problems and to sponsor programs which have temporary political significance rather than any longer-range importance; the main criterion for planning activities being that of pleasing the "powers that be."

The planning agency in the main stream of political and administrative activity so that plans and programs get carried out, but the chief executive relying on the planning agency to provide a framework for all improvement programs and development activities without getting involved in the short-run partisan activities.

The activities of the planning agency centering on a few clearly defined functions, such as the periodic revision of the master plan and the annual preparation of a capital budget and revision of a longer-range financial plan. The activities would involve regularized tasks, parts of which can be made routine—thereby using less expensive and more readily available skills.

The planning agency carrying out routine administrative tasks, which are mostly "busy work" carried out without significant reference points or in a vacuum, such as continual zoning changes, "quickie" studies, and reports on small-project plans.

The planning agency, as a staff unit, "co-ordinating and integrating" the programs of the various municipal departments where they involve the physical development of the city, but having no general framework by which to judge and merely trying to substitute one judgment for another (and generally more expert) one.

The planning agency providing a framework for the programs of the individual departments—in the form of master-plan standards and strategy —so that departmental programs can be geared to these in the first place and so that there are definite criteria for judging the recommended programs of the operating departments.

What emerges especially is the need for chief executives and political leaders of municipal governments to learn to use staff work, and specifically planning staff work, with some effectiveness. This is likely to take some time under any circumstances, but probably much less time if the city planners themselves have come to understand what is desirable—through appropriate university training as well as on-the-job experience. They can then, at least, advance a desirable pattern when the circumstances are favorable for organizational and administrative improvements.

ANOTHER TREND: GROWTH OF URBAN
AND REGIONAL STUDIES AND SPECIALIZATIONS

I have already referred to the various types of social science studies and research activities that have influenced city planning. It is worth noting also that simultaneously a group of specialists have been trained, within different academic disciplines, who are expert in various phases of urban living and metropolitan development.

Thus, members of the sociology departments of U.S. universities are carrying out studies and developing techniques of great importance for city planning; and they are also training urban sociologists, demographers and human ecologists, and other specialists who might conceivably play an important professional role in city planning. Similarly, political science departments are training public administrators and others who could become even more important in city planning than they already are. Economics departments and business schools are providing land economists, experts in aggregate economics (income, input-output, economic base studies, etc.), students of industry, transportation and marketing, and others. Departments of geography are training urban geographers, transportation experts, resources experts, and other specialists with advanced knowledge in the urban and regional fields. Similarly, there are property lawyers, specialists in laws regulating land uses, and others from the legal profession; cultural anthropologists from anthropology; social psychologists and others from psychology; and so on.

While more and more of these specialists have been seeking and finding employment in city planning, entrance of these groups into the planning field is still fairly limited. Here, again, is a great challenge for the planning schools—a challenge which, with only two or three possible exceptions, they are not meeting.

The city planning field has been developing in such a way that there is an ever-increasing need for skills of the type represented by the specializations referred to above. To take full advantage of the potentialities inherent in this situation, however, two requirements would have to be met. One is to attract some of the ablest of the individuals in these specialist groups into the planning field. This can be done most effectively at the university level, before they have finally decided on their career lines, rather than by planning agencies after they have been graduated. Only a planning school that has academic status, a broad-gauge program with many interdepartmental ties, and an important program of research, can hope to attract such people. The other requirement is that once it has attracted them, the planning school should be in a position to provide a significant training program in planning with a relatively small number of courses and workshops. Since planning studies would be a "minor" for these people, they cannot be expected to neglect their other studies to take a long period of training in planning. An extension of time for the total program of graduate studies is, of course, an attractive solution—but extremely difficult to apply in reality.

Another point which should be made in connection with these specialized skills is that recruitment of able persons from these groups might well be one of the most important steps in any program aimed at solving the current shortage of personnel in the planning field. Almost any other relatively short-run solution of the "supply problem" would tend to involve a lowering of standards in one form or another. It is not possible to argue logically that it is better to bring in poorer "general" planners—or rapidly and continually to upgrade partially trained and inexperienced "general" planners (so that they perform about as well as unseasoned wood in a frame structure)—rather than to recruit able specialists possessing skills much needed in city planning. Experience has shown that many members of these specialist groups tend to be attracted to city planning once they have come into contact with it. If they can be provided with a relatively brief "core" training in planning, they would make excellent recruits for both the public agencies and the private consultant groups.[22]

22 Those who are acquainted intimately with these specialist fields, as well as with city planning, tend to feel that these fields provide excellent preparation for a career in city planning, in both a specialist and in a general-planning

The great reservoir of skills and talents available in these city-oriented fields is a significant resource for city planning, a resource which is as yet largely untapped. The effective use of this resource should become a first order of business for the planning profession and, more particularly, for the planning schools.

IV   Foundations of Education
for City Planners

The progress of a profession usually depends upon many factors. Key among these is the extent to which the profession comes to base its techniques of operations upon principles rather than rule-of-thumb procedures or simple routine skills.[23] The more

---

role. Howard K. Menhinick, head of the planning school at the Georgia Institute of Technology, highlighted this point through the publication of an ingenious series of leaflets prepared by experts from various fields. Here are some of the comments of several of the experts.

Attorney Norman Williams, Jr.: "Lawyers have always played a prominent role in the development of urban and regional planning, and legal training provides several important advantages as a background for graduate study and a career in city planning."

Economist Alvin H. Hansen: "There seems . . . to emerge an attractive career in city planning for competently trained economists primarily interested in economic policy and community progress."

Sociologist Edwin S. Burdell: "Planning in a democratic society includes as much the organization of the community and the body politic, the means of mass communications, and the legislative and administrative processes as it does the specific physical solutions. In this whole process the sociologist can play a vital and creative role."

Other representatives from the social sciences were from business administration, geography, and public administration. Represented also were *architect* Henry S. Churchill, *civil engineer* Harland Bartholomew, and *landscape architect* S. Herbert Hare, and their statements about their fields as a preparation for city planning are as pertinent as the statements of the social scientists. However, I assume that it is not necessary at this stage to argue the case for using specialists from these fields in city planning.

23 For a useful discussion of this and other characteristics of a profession which set the fundamental tasks of professional education, see Ralph W. Tyler, "Distinctive Attributes of Education for the Professions," *Social Work Journal*, Vol. 33 (April 1952), pp. 55–62.

complex the problems with which the practitioners have to deal
and the greater the variety of situations they can expect to en-
counter, the more inadequate becomes the apprenticeship system
of education—whether the "master" transmits his accumulated
knowledge in a classroom or directly on the job. The major task
of professional education thus becomes one of developing and
advancing the basic principles to be used in the profession and
providing an integrated set of learning experiences which would
permit the student, in essence, to rediscover these principles himself and learn to apply them in a problem-solving setting.

The progress of a profession would also seem to depend on the
ability of the practitioners to relate themselves effectively to the
broader social and intellectual context within which they are
functioning. Thus, a sense of social responsibility (or what some
would call a code of ethics), high standards set and accepted for
research and articles in professional journals, and an ability to
exchange ideas and to work effectively with people from a variety
of fields—all these, and similar elements, tend to determine the
stature and the status of a profession.

One other point should be added. As a profession expands its
knowledge and skills, it finds that it must develop specialists of
all types if it is to make optimum use of the existing knowledge
and if it is to speed the development of additional knowledge
and skill.

These requirements for progress in turn suggest certain requirements with regard to professional education—for city planning as much as for other professional activities: (1) the need for
a sound general education as a foundation for professional education; (2) the need for professional schools to develop and emphasize the fundamental principles upon which the professional
tasks are based rather than rule-of-thumb procedures, and to
teach these principles so that they are understood in a broad
social and intellectual context as well as in a problem-solving
context; and (3) the need to cope with the problems of increasing
specialized knowledge and techniques by training not the narrow
specialist but the "generalist-with-a-specialty." [24]

[24] These requirements, in the broadest sense, are coming to be widely accepted by educators and practitioners in a variety of applied fields. See, for
example, the discussion by the members of the round table on "University

These might well be the guiding principles in the education of planners. Using such a standard, it seems evident that planning education in the United States has a long way to go before it can hope to provide a sound background for effective professional performance. Certain requirements would seem to be basic if the planning schools are to provide good professional education.

REQUIREMENT 1: GENERAL EDUCATION

First, the planning schools should require a general education at the college level of all those who will enter the field as planning professionals.

Reference to a "general education" does not imply any specific set of courses or even a specific approach to education. As a matter of fact, different colleges and universities use the term to cover what is in effect a wide variety of educational programs.[25] But there are important elements of agreement as to objectives and even program; thus, for example, general education is taken to include bringing the student into contact with the major academic fields (the biological, physical, and social sciences, and the humanities) as well as with certain tools of communication and thought such as English, foreign languages, and mathematics. It is agreed that the emphasis should be on the learning, thinking, and problem-solving processes so that, among other objectives, the student is provided with both materials and procedures for continuing lifetime learning.

From the standpoint of planning education, interest centers, of course, on the student having a broad foundation for training in city planning. A liberal arts education in the better colleges and universities would seem to meet the key requirement. Where the undergraduate curriculum in the college involves a great deal

Training for Administrative Duties," at the 1955 Session of the International Institute of Administrative Sciences, as reported in *Progress in Public Administration*, No. XII (August 1955), pp. 1–3.

[25] A valuable analysis of general education has been provided by the Committee on the Objectives of a General Education in a Free Society, *General Education in a Free Society* (Cambridge: Harvard University Press, 1945).

of specialization, however, much can be said for incorporating an undergraduate program in planning—essentially as a technique for broadening the educational base of those who want to become professional planners.[26]

The major problem today arises in the case of students whose undergraduate training is limited almost entirely to architecture, landscape architecture, or engineering, wishing to enter a graduate program in city planning. Here I would applaud Professor Adams' statement, in his report *Urban Planning Education in the United States,* to the effect that:

> The pattern now prevalent of superimposing two years of graduate work on to a four- or five-year course in a field other than planning [say, architecture or engineering] is open to serious question unless specific requirements in . . . general education are insisted upon at entrance to the graduate program or made additional to the two years of professional studies. In any event, every effort should be made to bring about greater coordination between the undergraduate and graduate curricula for those wishing to enter the planning field.[27]

A great deal of educational skill and imagination would be involved in working out programs in general education for students with undergraduate degrees in applied fields. A planning school would be well advised to try to obtain the assistance of professional educators—and especially those with substantial experience in the field of general education—in outlying programs for such students.

REQUIREMENT 2: A PLANNING "CORE"

The planning schools of the country should make a major effort to develop a sound planning "core" in their training programs. It may well be that this is the most important single requirement in the field of planning education at the present time.

[26] The inherently broad character of training in planning is given as one of the major reasons for the desirability of undergraduate education in city planning by Lloyd Rodwin, "The Achilles Heel of British Town Planning," Appendix A of *The British New Towns Policy* (Cambridge: Harvard University Press, 1956), pp. 196–97.

[27] Adams, *op. cit.,* p. vii.

A deliberate effort must be made to speed the development of general principles of city planning (in terms of substantive materials, hypotheses, and theories) as well as the development of basic methodology of planning. These basic principles and methods or techniques should make up the heart of the training program in planning—or, more accurately, should form the foundation for more specialized training in planning and for the continuing process of learning which should take place on the job.

A core program of training, which is developed specifically as the foundation for effective problem-solving and lifetime learning in a given professional field, obviously cannot be made up of a series of "survey" courses, or "cram" courses, or any other potpourri of courses. And this is as true of planning as of other professional fields. City planning has much to learn from other fields of study, but a sound planning education cannot be provided by exposing a student to bits and pieces of many subjects, given in the different departments and schools, as is done today by many of the planning schools. He should, of course, take courses —possibly a substantial number of courses—in other departments and schools, but these should be directly integrated into his basic training or specialized training, and not be merely a matter of "coming into contact" with a field which is "related" to planning. To say that a planner should have "a broad education" is not to mean that his education must cover everything, since that can be done only in the most superficial way, if at all.

A core program should center about the basic principles and methods of planning (which, one soon finds, are quite limited in number and scope). It should permit or encourage the student to rediscover the validity of the basic propositions by painfully struggling through the hypotheses and attesting to them himself— since this is the only way he will really come to understand them and be able to use them. Similarly, he should learn to use the basic methods by employing them in a problem-solving context. It is the thinking through and working through that is at the heart of the learning process, but of course the student must be provided with some materials, or intellectual building blocks, to work with—basic substantive materials, propositions, and techniques that others have worked out and that the student can build upon. The core program should serve other purposes as well. It should make it possible for the student to become acquainted first-hand with the primary materials and primary sources. It should enable him to come to understand various kinds of interrelationships—among problems, subject matter, specialists. It should help to develop in him basic attitudes and approaches to the planning field (such as a sense of social responsibility, appreciation of the possibilities and importance of creative solutions, humility as to what one man can know and what one group can accomplish and willingness to turn to others for help, to mention a few). In other words, the core program should provide a sound base on which advanced, more specialized, and lifetime planning education can be built.

This is not to suggest that the core program is the whole of a desirable curriculum in planning. Within a two-year graduate program in city planning, for example, no more than one year—and possibly somewhat less—would, I should think, be devoted to the core as such, although certain of the objectives would, of course, permeate the whole training program. The non-core courses would tend to be planning courses of a more detailed and specialized variety as well as courses in other departments and schools. These non-core courses can be expected to make up an important part of any curriculum, but they should—ideally—be the "superstructure" on a foundation of a planning core.

The planning core, if it is well conceived in terms of fundamentals, should serve almost equally well the educational needs of planners whatever their career lines—whether they will work for public planning agencies, or will come to be consultants chiefly working under contract with official agencies, or will serve mainly as consultants to private construction corporations or other private units. All of them must be well trained in the basic principles and methods; all of them must have a common language since they will have continual work contacts; all of them should share the responsibilities of the profession and, desirably, should also share certain attitudes, particularly as regards public responsibility and public service.

In order to provide a fuller explanation of this rather critical question of a planning core, some concrete suggestions concerning the possible content of such a core are set down in table 3.

It should be stressed that this is meant to be suggestive, rather than a specific proposal.

One of the main objectives of the suggested core program is to provide a technique for bringing together into a fruitful amalgam the two streams of development that have characterized city planning in the United States. Such an amalgam would mark the evolution of a new type of city planning profession (in fact, of a new type of profession)—one which effectively combined general administrative-political knowledge and a spirit of public service together with substantive skills related to the physical-socio-economic development of urban communities.

The content of the core curriculum must develop out of the requirement that the planner must learn to deal effectively with complex, relatively aggregate elements and interrelationships in a highly dynamic context—the evolving urban community. The planner is usually concerned with complex phenomena—such as the relation of homes to places of work and recreation—and with the physical, psychological, social, economic, and political aspects of any environmental or developmental problem or situation, and not just one aspect. He cannot retreat to *ceteris paribus* assumptions, as can the theoretical scholar. A fruitful way of learning to deal with aggregates and complex interrelationships is to learn to relate problems to a useful reference system or subject cluster. Four such clusters make up the first part of the illustrative core curriculum presented below.

TABLE 3   *Illustrative Content of a Planning Core Curriculum*

Outline of Key Elements Involved
    I. BASIC KNOWLEDGE: hypotheses, theories, principles—main focus on
        A. The Planning Process
        B. Urbanism and the Urbanization Process
        C. Physical Elements of Planning
        D. Socio-economic Elements of Planning
    II. BASIC METHODS AND TOOLS:
        A. Analytical
        B. Design
   III. PROBLEM-SOLVING EXPERIENCES:
        A. Case Studies and Individual Problems
        B. Group Workshop Problems

I. BASIC KNOWLEDGE (The four main foci represent groups of subjects which
are closely interrelated; planning core courses would not necessarily be
organized along this line).
  A. *The Planning Process:* some key topics—
     1. How planning fits into the decision making and operations of a cor-
        porate organization (private and public); staff and line functions,
        policy formation and administration, etc.
     2. Steps in the planning process; analysis of each step in the planning
        process in terms of the organizational context and the societal con-
        text (e.g., role of public, legislature, executive, staff offices, and line
        offices in establishment of goals, in choosing among alternative
        means, etc.)
     3. Major decision-making groups affecting development of urban com-
        munity: characteristics of these groups and how they are and can
        be influenced (e.g., the private builders, subdividers and bankers,
        construction unions, industrialists making location decisions, and
        so on).
     4. Uses and limitations of knowledge in planning; facts and values;
        functions of research and judgment.
     5. Standards, requirements, and priorities in planning.
     6. The organization of a public planning agency: alternative possibili-
        ties; relation to municipal departments; the nature of planning
        staff work; possible lines of communication with public, legislature,
        executive.
     7. The nature of planning decisions in private units concerned with
        urban development.
  B. *Urbanism and the Urbanization Process* (The focus is the urban com-
     munity and its development. Should provide a view of urbanization
     as a dynamic process related to developments in the economy, in tech-
     nology, in social organization, etc.). Some key topics—
     1. Historical development of cities; factors that have determined loca-
        tion, form, growth or decline.
     2. Relation to economic system: economic functions, relations to
        regional and national economy, economic base, interurban flows.
     3. Population growth and the pattern of movements in, into, and out
        of cities.
     4. Role of technology in urban development; forces involved in appli-
        cation of known technology, implications of new technology.
     5. Metropolitan structure: land uses under different types of urban
        organization, location of activity centers, nature of circulation sys-
        tems linking areas.
     6. Municipal and metropolitan government: forms and functions,
        trends in governmental changes and forces behind them; influence
        of government on urban development—past, present, and future.
     7. Efforts to plan and control the environment, from ancient times to
        present: varying goals and objectives, role of various power groups,

how man has organized to influence the environment, what has been legislated for (what problems urbanites have been most interested in solving) and what types of tools have been used. In general, what can be learned from the efforts of the past and present.

C. *Physical Elements of Planning* (The focus is the three-dimensional city, and movement of persons and things.)

1. Understanding the physical environment of the urban community: role of natural resources and physical factors in location, form, land use, density, and growth; land, water and other requirements of urban uses as compared to agricultural, recreational and other uses; potentialities of changes in physical features and physical limitations of a given environment, etc.

2. The theory of city form; major elements in the three-dimensional city. ✦

3. The major determinants of land use in the urban community and the principles of planning for land-use requirements, in alternative forms.

4. Key principles of intra-urban and inter-urban movement; transportation as a factor in urban growth and urban structure.

5. Utilities and facilities: interrelationship, location and design; the criteria of a well-serviced community.

6. Shelter in its various forms: the implications of current standards; the potentialities of existing and new technology; the context of shelter.

7. Esthetics: basic elements, changing popular taste, the social role of the designer and planner; the nature of creativity.

D. *Socio-economic Elements of Planning* (The focus is society and human behavior as it relates to planning in the urban community. Not a survey of the social sciences, but certain basic knowledge and approaches of these disciplines from the point of view of the planner and the problems he deals with, rather than that of the specialist in the discipline.)

1. Culture and personality: key factors in human behavior as they touch upon such matters as decision making, goals implicit in the culture, types of controls that tend to be resisted, types of problems for which solutions are collectively sought.

2. The nature of social institutions, particularly those geared to the solution of social problems, to reform, and to the furthering of special interests.

3. Economizing: the basic principles of deciding, in both public and private decision making, among alternatives on the basis of costs and returns (e.g., cost-benefit analysis in the evaluation of public works).

4. Power structure and power use in the community as it influences urban planning.

5. "Social engineering": the potentialities and limits of planned, rational action; the nature of social control.
6. The type of knowledge that the social sciences can provide about urban phenomena and rational group action, and how one can tap this knowledge.

II. BASIC METHODS AND TOOLS (Prerequisite: training in statistics, and in maps and aerial photographs).
   A. *Analytical Methods and Tools*
      1. Preparation and uses of physical survey and social survey in planning.
      2. Other techniques for analyzing current and evolving situations: e.g., economic base study, industry linkage and impact studies, techniques for analyzing traffic movement, etc.
      3. Use of models: mathematical, statistical, three-dimensional.
      4. Projection and prediction; dealing with situations of uncertainty.
   B. *Design Methods and Tools*
      1. Study of the key design features of cities, from ancient times to present, and of the basic techniques behind them.
      2. Design considerations in site planning.
      3. Basic elements of project design for different purposes (residential, commercial, industrial, civic, etc.); the development project under different circumstances (on new land, clearance and redevelopment, renewal—including rehabilitation and remodeling).
      4. Design elements in the neighborhood, the local community, the total urbanized area.

III. PROBLEM-SOLVING EXPERIENCES
   A. Use of case studies and of hypothetical problems wherever applicable, as a means of having the student work through principles and basic methods himself.
   B. Student workshops, applying planning and other knowledge and methods to the solution of planning problems and the preparation of plans. Workshop activity directed at: learning to work in a problem-solving context, learning to divide up tasks so that they become manageable, learning to use research in the analysis of problems and in the search for solutions, learning to measure the costs as well as the benefits of alternative solutions, highlighting the types of expertise needed in planning and how to obtain help (useful to call in local specialists to help with workshop problems), and, in general, development of attitudes and approaches to the planning field.

The above listing is intended only to highlight some key features of a planning core, and is meant to be only illustrative. A great deal of conscious effort on the part of many planning scholars and practitioners will be required before a really sound core based on planning principles and basic methodology can be developed. At this stage in the development of the planning profession, research by faculty members of planning schools on "core" subjects—that is, on the working out of principles and basic methods—will advance the planning field more than will research on peripheral and highly specialized aspects of planning.

Even assuming that very rapid progress can be made within the next decade on the working out of basic planning principles and methods, through a concerted and co-ordinated inter-university effort, it still cannot be expected that a uniform system of core courses will be established at all the planning schools— nor would it be desirable that this be done. There are many ways of opening up vistas for students through which they can come to understand, and learn to use, basic principles and methods, and it is highly desirable that various schools experiment with different approaches to the development of a core program. However, it *is* extremely desirable that methods of evaluation be devised so that the elements of strength and of weakness in the teaching program at each school can be known and improvements made over time. There are many ways of providing for such evaluation.[28]

Not only is the development of a planning core essential for the training of city planners, but the planning core may well be a lever to make possible the absorption into city planning of a large number of specialists from other fields. A real challenge for the planning school is to develop a planning core so attractive that

[28] One method which might be effective would involve an annual contest for the best solution of a common workshop problem drawn up by a contest-and-evaluation committee composed of experienced educators and practitioners. The students in the second-year workshop in each school would spend a specified period of time in working out a solution for the common problem distributed by the committee. These would be judged by the committee and a prize awarded for the best solution. In addition, the committee would set down detailed comments on each of the group solutions, pointing to good and weak elements of the solution. These comments should be helpful to the faculty of the various schools in coming to see gaps and weaknesses in their preparation of the students. The committee should be changed frequently, not only to avoid too great a burden on one group, but in order to get a variety of approaches represented over time.

able students from all over the university take the core courses and become potential recruits for city planning jobs.

REQUIREMENT 3: SPECIALIZED TRAINING

The final point suggested by a review of the key elements of professional education concerns specialization. Professional specialization appears to be inevitable, in planning as in other fields.

There is a strong tendency in certain of the planning schools today to attempt to train *the* planner. This stems from a feeling on the part of the faculty of these schools that a quite unique type of training of a generalist character is essential for city planners. Looked at in terms of the historical development of the planning profession, this approach can be seen as a rather natural —and healthy—reaction to the earlier educational background of city planners, which consisted of training in architecture, engineering, or other specialized fields, with, at best, only a few miscellaneous courses in planning. It has been important to establish that while in the past, when public works and land-use controls were almost the entire preoccupation of city planners, able individuals with nothing but a specialist background could perform effectively in the planning field, today the highly complex tasks of city planning call for graduate training in urban planning as such. Architecture, engineering and other applied fields, it is felt by most planning educators, may themselves be of "technical assistance" to city planning, but training in these fields involves materials, approaches, and methods which are substantially different from those involved in urban planning. Such specialist training, in reality, requires retraining if the individual is to be a good city planner.

Thus, the association between separate training in city planning and generalist training—or the training of *the* planner—may well arise from the conscious or subconscious need to set off planning training as such from specialist training in the applied fields as preparation for city planning careers.

It may be that this type of emphasis is still needed in order firmly to establish the separate and distinct character of the city planning field. But perhaps a better approach would be one less concerned with symbols and contrast and more concerned with the realities of quality. Such an approach would involve a conscious effort to bring about general improvement in the education provided in the planning schools. There is no better way of advancing the status of a profession than by the excellence and expertise of its specifically trained practitioners.

From this standpoint, I believe that it is a mistake for the planning schools to attempt to train *the* planner. At best, they will train individuals who will ultimately do well as top administrators, but will have had tough sledding in the early stages of their careers. At worst, they will train amateurs instead of professionals.

Given the complexity of modern city planning, some degree of specialization seems inevitable. But there are different approaches to specialization and different degrees of specialization. It is one thing to put a young person into a specialized field from the very beginning of his college training and never provide opportunities for a broadening experience. It is a very different thing to provide special advanced training to a student who has had a rich varied background provided by a general education and a well-developed planning core program. The objective for planning education seems clear enough. It is to provide *expertise with breadth of outlook.* This can be done by encouraging the student to build a "planning specialization" through a carefully devised program to meet his special needs and aptitudes after he has had his general education and his planning core, or parallel to these. (Specialized studies might quite effectively be taken at the same time as the more generalized studies.) I would call a person who has had this type of training a "generalist with a specialty," as contrasted with either the "pure" generalist or the specialist as such.

The key criterion is, of course, which type of university training will provide the best foundation for the important and long period of learning which will take place on the job. There is much to be said for training that will permit an individual to make significant contributions through his advanced knowledge of an important special field, as well as through his ability to handle a variety of problems wisely. C. R. Van Hise expressed this idea effectively in his much quoted AAAS speech, when he said: "No man may hope for the highest success who does not continue special studies and broadening studies to the end of his career."

A planning specialization can most effectively be developed on the basis of a full program of training—undergraduate as well as graduate. Thus, for example, a planning student who has had a substantial amount of training in the social sciences while an undergraduate, might well take some advanced courses in statistics, population and human ecology, and survey techniques (while he is taking his planning core as well as later) and then do a special piece of research on *social survey for planning*—thus developing, in a logical sequence, a useful specialization which will stand him in good stead in his planning work. Similarly, a planning student who has taken an undergraduate degree in civil engineering, might take advanced courses in subjects dealing with transportation (in the business school and in the department of geography, as well as in the engineering school and in the planning school) during and after his planning core training, and thus develop a specialization in *transportation planning*. Other needed planning specializations can be developed in a like fashion. Ideally, the specific planning specialization taken by a student should reflect: (1) the evolving needs of the planning field; (2) the interests and aptitudes of the student; (3) the educational background of the student; and (4) the areas in which the university can provide specialized training of a high order.

It would seem extremely difficult to achieve the goal of breadth combined with expertise unless the planning schools themselves concentrate on one element—or a very few elements—within the complex planning field. This is not to suggest that other elements should be neglected—far from it; the core elements must be taught, or the educational program would be incomplete. But I am firmly convinced that planning education will make genuine progress only when the various planning schools concentrate on those elements in which they have unusual strength all around.

What the appropriate "concentration" for a planning school might be would depend, of course, on its special areas of academic strength as well as on the nature of the tasks planners are called upon to perform—plus, one would hope, continual experiments in methods of training students characterized by "breadth-with-expertise." In the case of the very largest and strongest universities, more than one kind of concentration might be feasible, but the number of concentrations is not nearly as important as is the effort to be absolutely first-rate in whatever fields are taught. Illustrations of the kinds of concentrations that might be appropriate for various universities are:

1. Three-dimensional Urban Design (civic design, community architecture)
2. Construction and Transportation (planning of housing, urban utilities and facilities, and transportation)
3. Planning Administration and Planning Law
4. Socio-economic Analysis and Research

Thus, for example, planning schools located in technical institutes might be expected to concentrate on the first and/or the second of these to take advantage of their special strength, while a school in a university with a good social science faculty might concentrate on socio-economic research and analysis or on planning administration, or on both. But whatever the area of concentration, each planning school should be in a position to offer a strong, rounded core curriculum—otherwise it has no right to offer graduate degrees in planning.

If a planning school can cover everything and still be absolutely first-rate, it would have every justification in claiming to provide "a complete training in city planning." (It should still, of course, encourage its students to develop a planning specialization for themselves.) However, if a planning school does not have the resources to provide top-quality training in all fields of city planning, then it should consider very seriously the possibility of achieving higher quality by some form of concentration.

It might be objected that a development of the type suggested here would really be retrogression and that planning would once again tend to be a mere adjunct of a school of architecture or engineering or social science. If this were to be the consequence, then it would be retrogression indeed. Note, however—and this is the heart of the whole matter—that I have strongly stressed, throughout, the importance of a general education as an essential foundation and of planning training that centers on a carefully

worked out planning core. Both of these elements were missing
in the earlier period when planning *was* a mere adjunct of a
school of architecture, of landscape architecture, or of engineering. To go to the other extreme and remove planning education
entirely from the academic and professional fields which nourish
it, is just as much of a mistake.

The history of city planning and of the forces influencing it
suggests strongly that the very nature of city planning is such that
it can gain the most by continually nourishing itself by intimate
contact with related fields of study and of endeavor. It can do
this best *not* by trying to encompass everything (on the surface,
a foolish task), but by having as practitioners persons who are
"generalists-with-specialties" and who form a natural bridge to
the other "nourishing" fields.

The larger public planning agencies, particularly, need planners with substantial knowledge and skill in the major areas of
planning if these agencies are to get optimum returns from the
various specialists who are recruited into the planning agency.
Thus, for example, a planner with strong training in three-dimensional urban design can normally be expected to work more
effectively with the design technician than can the "complete
generalist," just as the planner who has developed a specialization in social survey for planning can work effectively with the
demographer brought in for a special study. Another way of put-
ting it is that the "generalist-with-a-specialty" is a natural link
between the administrators at the top of the governmental hierarchy and the various specialists who come from other fields.

A really effective and expert team can be built to carry out the
planning tasks by bringing together (1) planners with some specialized knowledge, (2) specialists with some training in planning,
(3) technicians to handle the purely technical tasks, and (4) individuals who do not fall into any particular category but because
of special attributes of talent and inclination can serve effectively
on a planning team. (There must always be room in planning for
the genuinely creative talent, whatever its background.)

TASKS OF LEADERSHIP

There seems to be a direct relationship between the maturity and progress of a profession and the amount of educational leadership provided by the full-time university scholars who devote themselves to the advancement of the field. The progress of the city planning profession during the next generation will depend to a significant degree on the extent to which the university educators can and do exert genuine leadership in planning education. This should involve advancement in a number of key areas:

1. *Recruitment.* The progress and the status of the planning profession are tied to the caliber and characteristics of the individuals who enter and stay in the city planning field. Leadership on the part of the planning schools in this area is urgently needed. The quality of the planning schools themselves is of course a crucial factor in recruitment: the attractiveness of the training program, the quality of the teachers, the interest aroused by the research activities, and the excitement generated by the planning schools in the academic world—all of these have a great deal to do with the number and caliber of students attracted into planning. Beyond this, the schools might contribute importantly to making potential recruits aware of, and interested in, the opportunities available in the city planning profession. There is a potentially great and rewarding field of endeavor here, and outstanding men and women must be challenged to enter the field and themselves make it possible for the potentialities to be achieved. There is an essential prior task of analyzing carefully and developing an understanding of the characteristics and aptitudes needed if an individual is to function well in city planning, and of the places (types of schools, academic fields, specific activities) where such characteristics and aptitudes, as well as potential interest, are likely to be found.[29] Recruitment, to be effective, must be purposeful and "pin-pointed."

[29] Dennis O'Harrow, Executive Director of the American Society of Planning Officials, underlined the importance of this type of study and analysis, in a letter to the author (of August 31, 1956), with a particular reference to the need for training a subprofessional group. He wrote:

"Dr. Edwin Burdell suggests that we must solve the shortage of planners (and of other professions) by recognizing and training a subprofessional group.

2. *On-the-job training.* The planning schools will have to come to play a central role in education beyond formal university training. A number of the larger public planning agencies have encouraged staff members to continue their studies and some have organized on-the-job training programs. To date, most in-service training programs have tended to be intermittent and fairly limited in scope. Educational leadership on the part of the planning schools would, certainly, involve assistance in the organization of regularized on-the-job training programs, supply of study materials, and provision of some of the teaching personnel.

3. *Lifetime education.* The question of encouraging lifetime learning, that is, of facilitating on the part of practitioners a continuing growth in knowledge, skills, and breadth of vision, is, of course, critical for educational leadership. There are many activities that can contribute to this general objective. The planning schools can encourage and, in the first place, inspire graduates to write for professional journals and to search for new knowledge and new methods in carrying out their tasks. They can sponsor summer sessions and special conferences (as two or three schools are already doing) and in other ways provide opportuni-

---

In all of the professions there will always be a limited number of persons who have the time, finances, and ability—especially ability—to complete a full course of training. Therefore we should consciously seek to set up courses and training for this subprofessional group. In medicine this group includes, of course, lab technicians, dental assistants, and practical nurses. In engineering it would include draftsmen, computers, surveyors, etc.

"From this beginning I would go on to say that perhaps we need some very careful management surveys of the activities in planning offices to determine how we can best train and supply subprofessional help to take care of the overwhelming problem of day to day planning administration. As every planning practitioner knows, all the creative planning that he can sandwich in between the demands on his time for zoning variances, subdivision review, house numbering, streets naming, and so on, will amount to practically nothing unless he has a much larger budget and staff than he can muster from the present and future supply of fully trained planners.

"And of course the matter of native intelligence and ability is quite important. There are many more persons competent to handle routine administrative problems than there are or ever will be to do creative planning. A good many of these less creative persons are even now in top jobs in planning staffs.

"I don't think we really know much about the duties, aptitudes, and quantity of personnel needed in the subprofessional group. I think this whole field could stand a great deal of study and investigation."

ties for practitioners to come *directly* into contact with new ideas, new methods, and new points of view. They might work to make the annual conferences of the professional organizations a useful educational device (as well as a meeting ground and a market place). They might do a great deal to contribute to the educational value of the periodic meetings of the local chapters of the professional societies and, even more importantly, to recruit local practitioners to assist in many ways in various educational tasks.[30] In general, the planning schools must become concerned with planning education in the broadest sense.

4. *Research.* The crucial present need is, as suggested earlier, the development through research—as well as in other ways—of the general principles and basic methodology of planning (concretely, in terms of evolving a sound core program). Close behind in importance comes research in significant new fields, the experimental areas. Both of these types of research, which will often tend to be interrelated, are needed not only to advance knowledge in city planning, but also as an important way of attracting really first-rate people into the planning field, as teachers, research workers, and practitioners.

5. *A program to speed educational progress.* It is apparent that there is now a ferment going on in the planning profession—among the practitioners as well as in the planning schools. The abler and more sensitive individuals in both realms are aware of a changing of directions, of exciting new opportunities just on the horizon, of glaring limitations in the profession which hinder progress. This may well be a situation not unlike the one which existed in 1928 when members of the planning profession and educators called a special conference to consider problems of planning education and research. Out of this conference came the first planning school in the United States and the start of a new era for the planning profession.

Today, as then, a great thrust forward in planning education is possible and called for. It will undoubtedly take the development, through the joint effort of leaders of the profession and university personnel, of a carefully worked-out program to speed

[30] In some communities the local professional chapter, because of the high caliber of its members, is in a position to contribute significantly to planning education.

progress in planning education, and possibly the winning of foundation support to help finance certain aspects of the program. Leadership by the planning schools in the design of such a program may well signalize the assumption of educational leadership by the university scholars. This would certainly be a development of great significance for the future of city planning.

Appendix I–A *Some Landmarks in the History of City Planning and of Planning Education in the United States* *

I. Earlier Phase

A. CHICAGO WORLD'S FAIR (1893) TO WORLD WAR I: *Main focus on "City Beautiful"; City planning instruction limited to lecture courses in a small number of landscape architecture schools.*

As a movement, city planning in the United States is usually thought to have started with the Chicago Fair.† Major emphasis was on esthetic considerations, but there was a growing awareness of social problems. Plans dealt mainly with civic centers, parks, streets, and transportation. They were sponsored by civic improvement organizations and prepared by consultants drawn chiefly from architecture and landscape architecture.

1893 Chicago World's Fair inspired civic efforts to improve the physical features of cities. Other civic movements coincided with the ferment stemming from the Fair and influenced city planning, e.g., the movement concerned with parks and natural areas (Charles Eliot's inspiring plan for the development of the Boston metropolitan park system was prepared in the early 1890's), the municipal reform movement, the home rule movement, and the settlement house and related movements which brought attention to slums, congestion, and similar social problems.

1902 Preparation of a revised plan for Washington, D.C., based on

* No attempt has been made to trace European and other outside influences (largely in the interests of brevity), even though in many instances these have been extremely important. The various periods cannot, of course, be set off sharply. Changes were gradual and there were important variations among the cities in stages of development as far as planning was concerned.

† Of course, American city planning goes much farther back, at least as far back as 1682 when William Penn laid out the checkerboard street system for Philadelphia.

the original L'Enfant Plan, by a committee of three architects and a sculptor who had been associated with the Fair.

1905   Organization of the National Association of Real Estate Boards, which, together with associations of private builders, bankers, and similar groups, has had a continuing influence on the course of city planning.

1907   Creation of first official city planning commission (in Hartford, Conn.).

1907   Publication of the *Pittsburgh Survey,* the first systematic city survey; included information on working conditions, housing and living conditions generally, hospital and other institutional needs of the city, and related questions.

1909   First National Conference on City Planning, sponsored by groups interested in better housing and sanitation, as well as by the professional societies of architects and landscape architects. The National Planning Conference—focal point of the organized planning movement—was actually organized in 1910 under the leadership of the architects and landscape architects.

1909   *Plan of Chicago,* sponsored by Commercial Club of Chicago, prepared by Daniel H. Burnham.

1909   Introduction of a lecture course on city planning at Harvard University for students in the department of landscape architecture. Shortly thereafter Charles Mulford Robinson introduced instruction in city planning into the landscape design curriculum at the University of Illinois.

1911   Publication of the *City Plan for Rochester,* prepared by Olmsted and Brunner, and George Kessler's *City Plan for Dallas,* together with the earlier *Plan of Chicago,* marked extension of the scope of city planning to a wide range of public improvements and to privately-owned transit and transportation.

B. WORLD WAR I TO LATE 1920's: *Main emphasis on zoning and on public-works and land-use planning (the "City Practical"); Instruction in city planning in schools of landscape architecture and architecture.*

City plans—usually referred to as "complete master plans"—were sponsored by semi-independent official city planning commissions (by the early 1920's there were almost 200 planning commissions), and prepared in the main by consultant firms. Plans usually treated streets, transit and other transportation, central business districts, public buildings, parks and recreation, "civic art or civic appearance," zoning and subdivision control. Emphasis was on the physical layout of the community, with detailed attention to the engineering and financial considerations.

1916   First comprehensive zoning ordinance, adopted by New York City.

1917   The American City Planning Institute was created, marking claim that practitioners considered city planning a separate profession. (Now the American Institute of Planners.)

1923   Wichita Plan, prepared by Harland Bartholomew and Associates, followed by the Memphis Plan (1924) and others typical of the period.

1923   The Department of Landscape Architecture at Harvard University introduced a graduate program leading to the degree of Master of Landscape Architecture in City Planning.

1924   Start of an extensive series of social science researches into the city and its problems at the University of Chicago under the auspices of the Local Community Research Committee (later the Social Science Research Committee).

1925   First plan to be officially adopted by the city council of a major city (Cincinnati).

1925   Inception of *The Journal of Land and Public Utility Economics* (now *Land Economics*) organ of the Institute for Research in Land Economics and Public Utilities founded by Professor Richard T. Ely of the University of Wisconsin.

1926   Supreme Court upheld comprehensive municipal zoning in a case brought from Euclid, Ohio—*Village of Euclid v. Ambler Realty Co.*, 272 U.S. 365 (1926), providing the "classic" statement in the field of zoning.

1927   Publication of the last edition of *A Standard State Zoning Enabling Act* and (in 1928) publication of *A Standard City Planning Enabling Act* (No. 5 and No. 11 of Building and Housing), Bureau of Standards, U.S. Department of Commerce. Both have greatly influenced state enabling legislation permitting municipalities to plan for and control the uses of land within their corporate areas.

1927   Radburn Plan adopted; first American "garden city" planned in an effort to achieve benefits of an integrated community; included planned use of the superblock with open space at the center and cul-de-sacs. In part, reflected the influence of Sir Ebenezer Howard's *Tomorrow* (published in 1898) and the ideas generated by the Garden City Movement.

1927   The pace of construction influenced the role of city planning in the 1920's. Around 810,000 housing units were constructed in urban communities during 1927, the peak of the housing boom.

Some 6,400,000 housing units were constructed during the decade
of the 1920's.

II. The Modern Phase

A. 1928–29 TRANSITION: *The culmination of developments of the earlier
phase in the history of city planning and the beginning of the modern phase.*

1928   Conference on instruction and research in city and regional plan-
        ning under the joint sponsorship of Columbia University and the
        Committee on Regional Plan of New York and Its Environs.
        Stressed the desirability of developing separate teaching and
        research facilities for "city or regional planning."
1929   Establishment of first school of city planning, at Harvard Uni-
        versity, with the financial assistance of the Rockefeller Founda-
        tion. Provided a three-year postgraduate course leading to a
        degree of Master in City Planning.
1929   Completion of the influential *Regional Plan of New York and
        Its Environs.* Emphasis was on economic, population, and govern-
        mental problems as well as on the more usual physical elements;
        also detailed consideration of the broader region as well as the
        core city.

B. THE 1930's: *Increasing attention to social problems in city planning;
Larger role of federal government in urban affairs; Separate graduate training in city planning.*

City planning in the 1930's was dominated by social and economic
surveys and by housing and slum-clearance projects, almost all carried
out with some federal aid. It was strongly influenced by the activities of
federal agencies such as the Federal Housing Administration, the
United States Housing Authority, WPA and PWA, and was aided by
the National Resources Planning Board and its predecessors. As compared with earlier planning there was greater interest in economic and
social problems, including the problems of the "lower third," and in
administrative problems relating to planning.

1930   Publication of "Harvard City Planning Studies" begun.
1931   The White House Conference on Home Building and Home
        Ownership. Publications of the Conference were widely used in

schools and had an influence on planning and housing thought.

1933 Establishment of the National Planning Board (successors: National Resources Board—1934–35, National Resources Committee—1935–39, National Resources Planning Board—1939–43) which encouraged and helped city planning in many ways.

1933 Inauguration of a five-year course leading to the degree of B. Arch. in City Planning in the School of Architecture at the Massachusetts Institute of Technology.

1934 First "real property inventories" and housing and urban-blight surveys. Also start of housing and slum-clearance projects carried out with federal aid.

1934 Formation of the American Society of Planning Officials. Its slogan: "To Promote Efficiency of Public Administration in Land and Community Planning."

1935 Start of M.I.T. graduate program in city planning, leading to a Master's degree; followed shortly thereafter by the establishment of planning schools at Cornell University (1935), with the aid of five-year grant from the Carnegie Corporation, and at Columbia University (1937).

1936 Over 900 official city planning commissions in existence; as well as over 500 county and metropolitan planning agencies. (The latter increased from 85 to 506 between 1933 and 1936.)

1937 Publication of *Our Cities: Their Role in the National Economy*, report of the Urbanism Committee of the National Resources Committee. Emphasized social and economic problems; relationships between the city, the state, the region, and the nation; need for federal assistance to lower units of government; and the desirability of a broad view of the functions and potentialities of planning.

1937 Publication of the report of the President's Committee on Administrative Management; was influential in advancing the view of planning as a staff function directly helping the chief executive. (Robert A. Walker, in his book *The Planning Function in Urban Government*, 1941, applied this concept to planning in municipal government.)

1938 New York City Planning Commission, under a new charter, began to operate under the broadest powers granted to any planning agency, including: adoption of a master plan, custody of city map, initiation of changes in zoning ordinance, and preparation of a capital budget which could be altered only by a three-quarters vote of the Board of Estimates.

C. 1940 TO PRESENT: *Increase in scope and areal extent of planning ac-*
tivities; Importance of federal aid, particularly in urban redevelop-
ment and renewal; Rapid increase in number of planning schools.

During World War II, city planning agencies provided some spot assistance to operating officials and, in some cases, prepared postwar public
works plans. Since the war, plans in the larger cities have been prepared
by technical staffs of official planning agencies with the help of consultants; plans in smaller towns have been chiefly prepared by consultants. Activities of most planning agencies have been focused on zoning
and subdivision control (taking 25 to 50 per cent of staff time), public
housing, redevelopment and urban renewal and transportation, with
increasing importance attached to capital programming. There has been
a great increase in planning activities carried out by private development companies, and by municipal public housing, redevelopment, and
renewal authorities. Also there has been a large growth of citizens'
groups interested in improvement of urban environment and neighborhoods. The number of degree-granting planning schools has increased
greatly since 1940, but the number of graduates has fallen short of the
job opportunities in the field.

1941   Publication of *A Handbook on Urban Redevelopment for Cities
        in the United States,* by the Federal Housing Administration,
        anticipating expansion of redevelopment activities with federal
        assistance.

1941   Establishment of three planning schools in one year (at the Uni-
        versity of Michigan, Illinois Institute of Technology, and Univer-
        sity of Washington), marking the beginning of the recent rapid
        growth in separate professional training for city planning. In
        1944, a planning program was established at the University of
        Wisconsin and in 1946 programs were started at the University of
        North Carolina and at Michigan State College.

1946   Beginning of Pittsburgh Golden-Triangle redevelopment project
        which served to emphasize the possibilities of urban planning
        and redevelopment and to inspire many community undertakings
        as well as many unfulfilled grandiose plans.

1947   Establishment of University of Chicago's Program of Education
        and Research in Planning, with emphasis on the social sciences,
        on research, and on regional considerations in planning. In the
        same year, planning schools were started at the University of
        Illinois, Rutgers University, and the University of Texas.

1947   Report on "The Content of Professional Curricula in Planning," drawn up by the Committee on Planning Education of the American Institute of Planning and adopted by the Institute, expressing something of a consensus of the more advanced professional view on planning education.

1947 First occupancy of Levittown, New York, followed by first occupancy of Park Forest, Illinois (1948), marking the beginning of the postwar "new town" mass-built housing boom. The development of new communities on a large mass-built scale, which had had important beginnings before and during World War II (e.g., Oak Ridge, Tennessee; Midtown, Oklahoma, etc.), gained momentum after the war.

1948 The University of California established a planning school, as did the University of Oklahoma and the University of Florida. This was followed by the establishment of planning programs at Iowa State College (1949), Yale University (1950), University of Pennsylvania (1951), the Georgia Institute of Technology (1952), and the University of Southern California (1955).

1949 The National Housing Act of 1949, providing funds for public housing and redevelopment, and reaffirming the principle that federally aided urban developments, whether undertaken as publicly owned units or as private redevelopment projects, should conform to a planned program for the entire community.

1954 The National Housing Act of 1954, introducing the "urban renewal" concept which includes neighborhood conservation and rehabilitation as well as redevelopment. A "Comprehensive Community Plan" is mandatory and a "Workable Program" is required for an urban area to qualify for federal financing. The federal government offered, under Sec. 701, to make money available, on a 50–50 matching basis, to state planning agencies for planning assistance to municipalities under 25,000 population and to official state, metropolitan, or regional planning agencies for planning work in metropolitan and regional areas. The 1956 Act broadens this section to include planning assistance to municipalities and counties of 25,000 population and over which are declared by the President to be "disaster areas."

SOURCES: Thomas Adams, *Outline of Town and City Planning* (New York: Russell Sage Foundation, 1935); Robert A. Walker, *The Planning Function in Urban Government* (Chicago: University of Chicago Press, 1941, revised edition, 1950); John M. Gaus, *The Education of Planners* (Cambridge: Harvard Graduate School of Design, 1943); Frederick J. Adams, *Urban Planning Education in the United States* (Cincinnati: Alfred Bettman Foundation, 1954).

Walker, particularly, gives an excellent account of the development of the modern planning movement in the United States. F. J. Adams provides a full picture of the situation in city planning education as of 1954. Because of the ready availability of such recent data on planning schools, it did not seem necessary to include here detailed descriptive materials on planning schools.

Appendix I–B *Intellectual and Professional Contributions to, and Influences on, City Planning* (Some Examples)

1. *From architecture, landscape architecture, art (and related fields) have come concepts concerned with* THREE-DIMENSIONAL URBAN DESIGN *(Civic Design, Community Architecture):* *

(a) The concept of an appropriate goal for design and planning as being a physical environment which is esthetically and in other ways humanly satisfying, imparting a sense of "wholeness," and providing for changes in keeping with the changing needs and values of the civilization.

(b) Site planning and project design as the design of spaces and structures within integrated units (projects) which meet biological, technical, economic, social and psychological requirements and demands.

(c) The spatial and three-dimensional elaboration of the concepts of the new town, the garden city, the neighborhood unit, the superblock and organized use of open space, giving specific (and inspirational) content to generalized concepts.

2. *From engineering and related fields have come concepts concerned with* FUNCTIONAL EFFICIENCY:

The most efficient and economical over-all arrangements for home and work activities, for movement of people and things, and for public

* There is no uniformly accepted term that can be employed to represent the contributions of those concerned with the design elements of the urban community, including the landscape architect, the architect, the student of fine arts, and the art historian, as well as the planner. The term "Civic Design" is widely and traditionally employed, particularly where a strong esthetic emphasis is involved. "Community Architecture" is a descriptive term employed by Clarence Stein, evidently intending both to convey the architect's claim to the field and to distinguish large-scale urban design from the design of individual structures (with the quite different skills involved). The term "Physical Planning" is sometimes used to connote urban design, but it is also used—at the other extreme—to cover all of city planning, and for that reason is an especially confusing term.

facilities and utilities. The concept of engineering and planning as seeking to produce social end-products at lowest possible cost.

3. LAW:

Planning as an aspect of the legal structure of the social system; development of the concepts of police power, eminent domain and related concepts involving public regulation and control of property and land use.

4. POLITICAL SCIENCE, PUBLIC ADMINISTRATION AND "MANAGEMENT":

(a) The concept of planning as an activity directly influenced by the power structure of the community.

(b) The concept of planning as increasing the efficiency and economy of government; also, planning specifically as an "overhead" staff function.

(c) "Scientific Management" and more recently "Operations Research": Integration of specialized operations and functions into a comprehensive whole on the most efficient possible basis, through scientific analysis of operations, scheduling and smoothing of flows, and optimum arrangements. (There has been an intermingling of ideas and influences concerning "management" in industry, military branches, and government.)

5. SOCIAL SCIENCE RESEARCH:

(a) Geographic and ecological studies of land as related to natural influences and to man and his "works"; development of techniques of land-use analysis.

(b) Land economics, including studies of supply and demand factors in the use and development of land and improvements and of property market behavior and what it takes to control such behavior.

(c) Economic studies (economic base, industrial location, markets, etc.) have provided information, tools and techniques for planning, and have highlighted the importance (1) of weighing costs and benefits of alternative proposals, (2) of strengthening the economy of the community, and (3) of considering the relationship of cities to other parts of the economy.

(d) Studies of policy formation and "decision-making" in government organizations.

(e) Social survey, including concept that city planning must be based on a thorough understanding of the total city and the dynamic social forces at work within the metropolis (e.g., population movements, migration, and other forces coming under the heading of "human ecology").

(f) Psychological and social studies of individuals and small groups; development of techniques for getting an understanding of individual and group needs, wants, aspirations, actions and reactions.

(g) Communications research, "action research," "human dynamics," and other studies concerned with ways of reaching people, getting them "involved," and "getting things done" have opened new vistas for ways of achieving effective planning.

(h) Studies and activities concerned with specific urban social problems, particularly housing, crime and delinquency, education, health, and welfare.

6. GOVERNMENT FINANCE:

(a) Municipal finance concepts, and particularly the capital budget, the long-range financial plan, the programming of individual projects, and in general the view of physical development and other planned activities as having a budgetary-cost consideration as well as space and time dimensions.

(b) Fiscal policy ideas and particularly the notion of planning with an awareness of the business cycle.

7. *From a number of fields have come contributions to* REGIONAL ANALYSIS AND PLANNING:

(a) The concept of the region as the basis for planning, in a variety of forms: for example, the "natural region," the city-region (the region as the area over which the urban influence extends), and other concepts emphasizing the importance of viewing the city in a broad context.

(b) Regional analysis, providing concepts, information, and tools being increasingly employed in city planning—for example, regional input-output analysis, industrial location studies, regional resource analysis, area income studies, etc.

(c) Concepts relating to state and regional economic development, and particularly the relation of city planning and development (e.g., industrial sites, adequate homes for workers, transportation) to the effort to strengthen the economy of an area. More generally, concepts concerning the relationship of urbanism to economic development.

(d) Metropolitan planning and functions; ideas concerning the planning and operation of specific activities on a metropolitan basis and the value of metropolitan (regional) planning organizations. Also, metropolitan government—the emphasis on the desirability for adjustment in governmental structure to meet the physical, economic and social realities.

8. PLANNING FOR SPECIFIC GOVERNMENTAL FUNCTIONS:

Knowledge and skills developed in various "operational" fields have influenced city planning in general, as well as the other way round, although the relation between city planning commissions and city departments is still on the fuzzy side. Possibly most important have been the influences stemming from the ideas and methods developed in departmental planning and operations of urban and intercity transportation, schools, health, parks and recreation, and agricultural land-use planning and zoning at the urban fringe.

PART II

Education for

Regional

Planning &

Development

I Evolution of Regional and State Planning

The term "regional planning" in the United States is applied to a broad range of activities in many kinds of geographic areas:

1. Planning tasks underlying the development and management of the water, land, and related natural resources of river basins and other "resources regions." The focus of such tasks might extend from a small watershed or forested region to the Tennessee Valley or the vast Columbia Basin.

2. Efforts to guide the over-all physical growth and development of the sprawling metropolitan or city-regions, particularly where consideration is given to the entire area under the influence of the central city, including the satellite industrial and

dormitory towns, the rural zones, and the drainage basin(s).

3. Planning underlying the construction and operation of various types of facilities or the management of certain services which, because of their technical character or for other reasons, are regional in scope. Included are: interurban highways, ports, and other types of transportation facilities, region-wide water and sewerage facilities, and so on. Planning activities of the Port of New York Authority are in this category.

4. Planning efforts directed at fostering the economic development of areas, including the promotion of industries. The "region" in this case may extend from a large multistate area (as is the case in the work of the New England Council) to a relatively small cluster of communities.

All of these are concerned with what are usually called "developmental" activities. As regional planning has been evolving in the United States, the major emphasis has come to be on the *physical and economic framework for productive activities and urban growth,* with a problem focus on economic and resources development. When effectively done, regional planning tends to provide a context for city planning and for individual projects such as water or land development projects.

Persons from a variety of disciplines and applied fields of study participate in regional planning—engineers, agronomists, foresters, city planners, economists, lawyers, public administrators, geographers, and others. Of the many working in the regional field, few have been trained specifically for careers in regional planning or for work in connection with economic and resources development, and there are a very limited number of positions in governmental or private organizations that make use of any of these terms in their titles.[1] Certainly there is no single and clear line of career approach for the regional planning field as a whole or for any important phase of it. Nor, given the diversity of the tasks involved in regional planning and development, is it conceivable that regional planning should be the focus for an exclusive separate profession.

[1] For a discussion of the diversity of the regional planning field, see John M. Gaus, "Education for the Emerging Field of Regional Planning and Development," *Social Forces,* Vol. 29 (March 1951), pp. 229–36.

It does not follow from this, however, that university education and research programs concerned with regional planning, regional economic and resources development, and regional studies are not strongly to be desired. Such programs, particularly if stemming from a strong research interest, could provide an interdisciplinary focus with intriguing academic possibilities and immediate practical significance.

The programs would encompass both basic research and a small number of graduate courses and seminars as *supplementary* education (or a "minor" field) for persons from various disciplines and professions who are already working in the regional field or who intend upon completion of studies to seek positions concerned with some phase of regional planning and development or related work.

Such university programs need not be concerned with regional planning exclusively. Regional planning logically emerges as one element in a broader field of either (a) planning studies or (b) regional studies.

A university program that is concerned with all types of *planning* problems could offer regional planning as one of the fields of concentration. Or within the framework of a broadly conceived field of *regional studies,* regional planning can be *one* of several closely related fields of interest and of career outlets. The fields having both close content and career relationship at the present time include the following: (1) natural resources (forestry, agronomy, etc.), (2) transportation, (3) area development, (4) some aspects of marketing, (5) state planning, (6) overseas technical assistance work in the regional field, and (7) regional research and regional studies as such. For all of these, *regional economic and resources development* tends to be the central "problem focus."

There are important reasons for considering the question of education and research programs in the regional field at the present time.

With the continuing shifts in the location and character of economic activities in the United States, and with the very rapid urbanization, there is need for more and firmer knowledge concerning the structure and functional relations of regions and of the forces critical in their growth. There is a specific need for learning a great deal more about making regional economic and demographic projections, particularly since many private and public decisions are inevitably based on assumptions about the future pattern of a region's growth. This is seen most sharply in the case of capital investment decisions. There are many other questions of practical as well as of theoretical and methodological importance—concerning natural resources, transportation patterns, intergovernmental relations, and so on—where knowledge can be advanced through research with a regional focus. Valuable work has been done along these lines over a long period of time and much additional regional research is now under way; but only a beginning has been made, and university research-and-education programs organized on a continuing basis could do much to advance this significant area of knowledge.

Regional planning and development activities—whether dealing with the orderly growth of a broad city-region, or with the multiple-purpose development and integrated management of a river-control system, or with the factors influencing the economic expansion of a depressed region—are by their very nature concerned with the *interrelation* of certain basic physical, economic, political, and social elements as they influence a broad range of private and public decisions. The education of persons who have, or will have, the responsibility for such activities can hardly be considered adequate unless they have had an opportunity to achieve an understanding of these forces through specially focused interdisciplinary study. Supplementary education of this type may well be one of the most effective ways of raising the quality and effectiveness of several closely related fields of endeavor which are important for the future of our society but which currently tend to be overspecialized.

The question of education for regional planning is approached here by way of a review of the history of regional and state planning and an analysis of the nature of the regional planning field as it has been evolving in the United States. Such an analysis helps to provide a picture of both the limitations and potentialities of the field, and gives a basis for understanding the educational requirements for work in regional planning and closely related fields. An examination of the existing regionally oriented training and research activities at U.S. universities, presented in the last section, suggests existing gaps—in terms of the requirements—and also some possibilities for developing strong regional programs based largely on present faculty strength and interest.

NATURE AND HISTORY OF REGIONAL PLANNING

Regional planning has evolved in a fashion quite different from that of city planning. In spite of many unresolved questions, city planning in the United States has emerged as a field of activity whose general scope and focus of interest are widely understood. It has for some decades provided well-established career outlets. It has also had a fairly clear-cut (even if dual) and cumulative line of development.

All these features have been different in the case of regional planning. In the first place, the regional planning concept is itself remarkably elusive. In the scholarly texts and in popular usage, as well as in practical affairs, "region" is a flexible, almost generic, term, and there is general agreement that specific designations of regions must vary according to the needs, purposes, and standards involved in the designation.[2]

2 For example, the Tennessee Valley Authority, logically enough, employs a different regional demarcation for the management of the water system and for its electric power service area (which extends over a much larger area than the former).

There have been some scholarly attempts to delimit the term "region," but with little discernible success as far as practical usage is concerned. The problems of defining and delimiting regions have occupied the attention of geographers from an early day, including Fenneman, Morse, and Smith in the United States, Vidal de la Blache in France, Herbertson and others in England. For a recent treatment of the subject, see *American Geography: Inventory and Prospect*, edited by P. E. James and C. F. Jones (Syracuse: Syracuse University Press, 1954), pp. 21–68. Howard W. Odum used the term "region" for the largest of a series of hierarchical designations only, with other terms for the smaller units; thus, the region, the district, the subregion, the state, and the zone. See "The Promise of Regionalism," *Regionalism in America*, edited by Merrill Jensen (Madison: University of Wisconsin Press, 1952), pp. 395–425. Bogue, working with others, has suggested a system for delimiting the "economic areas" of the United States, employing four hierarchical levels: economic provinces, economic regions, economic subregions, and state eco-

The complexity arising from variability in regional demarcation is compounded by the complications of governmental organization for carrying out regional planning and development tasks. It has long been apparent that where planning, to be effective, must cut across existing governmental boundaries, such planning in our existing system of government must usually be based upon state powers [3] or upon a combination of federal, state, and local powers. Thus, in many kinds of problems and activities—say, in planning the further development of a watershed in a metropolitan region, or planning for the physical and economic improvement of a depressed coal-mining region—state planning

nomic areas. See Donald J. Bogue, "An Outline of the Complete System of Economic Areas," *American Journal of Sociology,* Vol. 60 (September 1954), pp. 136–39.

The term "region" is frequently applied to groups of nations (e.g., Southeast Asia), as well as to parts of a single nation. Within a national context, the term is generally used to designate a part of the country which is larger than a locality and smaller than the total nation and which has specified characteristics: (1) of homogeneity, i.e., common physical, economic, or socio-cultural features, or a combination of these; (2) of nodality, i.e., functional integration of outlying areas and a central place or node, typified by the metropolitan region with its center, suburbs, and broad hinterland; or (3) of problem-and-decision interdependence, i.e., important common problems, kindred and interdependent interests, interrelated activities, and common organizations and institutions. This last view of the region is concerned with the elements determining the potentialities for group planning and action, and involves a particular kind of problem- and action-oriented homogeneity. See Joseph L. Fisher, "Concepts in Regional Economic Development," *Papers and Proceedings of the Regional Science Association,* Vol. 1 (1955), pp. W1–20. Valuable recent discussions of the regional concept are to be found in the works of Ackerman, Bogue, Colby, Florence, Friedmann, Garnsey, Gottman, Hagood, C. Harris, S. Harris, Hoover, Isard, James, Jones, Lösch, Mangus, Mumford, Odum, Platt, Vance, Whittlesey, Zimmerman, and others.

[3] In discussing the handling by government of subnational suprastate problems, the National Resources Committee, some two decades ago, pointed out: "The whole matter would seem to reduce to a somewhat paradoxical situation, viz.: That in the States and only in the States, reside many of those powers necessary to make planning and planned accomplishment a reality. At the same time, the problems to be treated do not follow State lines but resolve themselves into regional units, and hence do not often lend themselves to treatment by existing political arrangements." *Regional Factors in National Planning* (Washington, D.C., December 1935), p. 23. See also James W. Fesler, *Area and Administration* (University, Alabama: University of Alabama Press, 1949).

(and possibly federal, county, and city planning as well) will come into play, whether a specific regional program is evolved or not.

Add to this complication the fact that regional planning and state planning were rather hurriedly given concrete organizational form during the early New Deal period, only a relatively short time after they had emerged on the U.S. scene, and it is apparent why their development should have been anything but orderly and cumulative. Their history has been disjointed, and this has had a profound effect on the current structure—or, rather, lack of structure—of regional and state planning.

In broad strokes, this history can be said to have covered three stages: first, the period before 1933 when there were scattered, unrelated beginnings in regional and state planning; then a period of several years after 1933 when the states and the federal government set up many planning units concerned with a broad range of physical, economic, and social problems, and dedicated to a comprehensive approach in planning; and finally the postwar period, leading into the present, when federally oriented "comprehensive" planning was abandoned in favor of state and regional planning which, while fairly extensive, is essentially unrelated and without any commonly recognized focus.

THE EARLY PERIOD

Regional and state planning, like many other concepts and activities, are rooted far back in history, but the beginnings of what we now think of as regional and state planning date from the 1920's.[4] New York State, in 1923, set up a temporary Com-

---

[4] Important antecedents were the organization of the Geological Survey in 1879 and the work of John Wesley Powell in land classification as a basis for the distribution of public lands and for the planning of land use in the public domain. See Wallace Stegner, *Beyond the Hundredth Meridian: John Wesley Powell and the Second Opening of the West* (Boston: Houghton Mifflin, 1954). Also noteworthy was the Inland Waterways Commission report of 1908 which refined the concept of the multiple-purpose development of river basins. The National Conservation Commission and the Country Life Commission (1908–09), appointed by President Theodore Roosevelt, were also concerned with multiple-purpose development, management, and use of natural resources, as well as with problems of conservation. A detailed examination of the ante-

mission of Housing and Regional Planning which, in addition to its work in the housing field, was broadly concerned with problems of the state's economic development and with the need for a permanent central state planning agency. Its report of 1926 is usually cited as the first comprehensive state "planning" report.[5] Between 1929 and 1931 state planning agencies were established in New Jersey, Wisconsin, and Illinois. Much of the work of these agencies centered on promoting city and metropolitan planning within their states and on assisting local planning agencies.

A large number of state departments of conservation or of natural resources were established in the 1920's (a few, in fact, were set up between 1917 and 1919). Some of these agencies undertook regional planning in the course of their development and management functions, particularly in regard to land, forests, and recreational facilities. There were also beginnings in the

---

cedents of state planning—in the context of a discussion of state resource conservation activities—is to be found in Clifford J. Hynning, *State Conservation of Resources* (Washington, D.C.: National Resources Committee, 1939). Brief accounts of the growth of state planning are provided in the report of the National Resources Board, *State Planning* (Washington, D.C., June 1935); and in Albert Lepawsky, *State Planning and Economic Development in the South* (Washington, D.C.: National Planning Association, Committee of the South, Report No. 4, 1949).

[5] In a message to the state legislature, outlining a program of state administrative reorganization, Governor Alfred E. Smith in 1926 made the following noteworthy statement: "With the development of our great water power resources, our port facilities, and the tremendous growth of private industry, we feel the pressure of considering plans for the whole State that will relate all these activities effectively to one another. The State bureau of housing and regional planning has done pioneer work in this field, and I have no doubt that in the reorganization of the Government, regional planning will be provided in such a manner as to keep it in close contact with the executive branch of the Government, making use of the special knowledge of the department heads concerned and also of outside expert assistance." Quoted in Hynning, *op. cit.*, p. 15. The emphasis on the relation between planning and development, the suggestion of economic and resources development as a focus for state planning, and the appreciation of planning as a potentially important staff arm for the chief executive mark a propitious launching of state and regional planning. Unfortunately, this eminently sensible view of planning did not become the basis of state planning activities.

use of regional analysis in state-wide highway and public works planning.

Regional planning for river basin development likewise got a significant start in the 1920's. A background of basic data collection significant to later regional planning was provided for in the authorization by Congress (in acts of 1923, 1925, and 1927) of the so-called "308" surveys. These surveys were the first effort on the part of the federal government to appraise the water resources problems and potentialities on a watershed basis. They furnished the groundwork for the extensive river basin construction programs of the 1930's and after. Significant also was the interstate compact for the Colorado River, signed in 1922 following a survey of the Bureau of Reclamation, and the later construction of the Boulder (Hoover) Dam. In the late 1920's a number of Southern California communities joined together to sponsor regional plans looking to the provision of an adequate water supply for the region.[6]

Public economic development and promotion efforts began to receive increasing attention in state governments in the 1920's. For example, North Carolina set up a Department of Conservation and Development in 1925 whose function was "to point out in broad terms existing conditions for the guidance of trade bodies in promoting the growth of their communities and of the State at large." A similar agency was set up in Virginia in 1926 and a few other states followed suit in setting up state development commissions. Most of these, however, did not survive the onslaught of depression.

The metropolitan region also began to receive serious attention in the 'twenties. A Los Angeles County Regional Planning Commission was created in 1922 and the Allegheny County Planning Commission was given official status in 1923. The most ambitious step forward was taken in New York. A committee on the "Regional Plan of New York and Its Environs" was organized (in 1922) to carry out an extensive survey of the New York metropolitan region—covering a radius fifty miles from the center of

6 Cf. Vincent Ostrom, *Water and Politics: A Study of Water Policies and Administration in the Development of Los Angeles* (Los Angeles: The Haynes Foundation, 1953).

New York City—and to prepare a general plan. A series of survey volumes was published (in 1927–29) dealing with problems of population, industry and economic development, land values, government, public services and facilities, and metropolitan structure and growth. This pioneer group also sponsored, in cooperation with Columbia University, a conference on instruction and research in city and regional planning. The conference stressed the desirability of promoting teaching and research facilities for "city or regional planning." This conference had a great deal to do with the establishment in 1929 of the first planning school, at Harvard University, but the school concerned itself almost exclusively with city planning. The broader metropolitan region did not become a subject of planning study until much later.

The survey and planning reports of the Regional Plan of New York and Its Environs inspired similar work in the Philadelphia Tri-State area, and in the Chicago, St. Louis, Washington, Boston, and other metropolitan areas. Some of this metropolitan urban planning was organized on a county basis, as was some rural planning.

By the time the National Planning Board began to "cultivate and stimulate" a network of state and regional planning organizations tied in with the national relief and recovery programs, the United States had had only about a decade of relatively modest experience with regional and state planning.

THE NEW DEAL PERIOD

The National Planning Board was set up shortly after the Roosevelt Administration came into office to help in the preparation of a public works program under the direction of Harold L. Ickes. Its function was soon broadened to encompass national planning activities of a comprehensive sort. As its functions broadened, its name changed: from National Planning Board (1933–34) to National Resources Board (1934–35) to National Resources Committee (1935–39) to National Resources Planning Board (1939–43). Since many of the federal programs had to

be carried out through state powers or at least required state co-
operation, the national planning agency set about sponsoring the
establishment of state and regional planning boards ". . . to
make plans within the framework of the national program." It
did this by calling the attention of state officials to the possibilities of financing state planning under the emergency relief grants.
The response of the states was immediate and all but one state
(Delaware) set up an official planning agency by act of the legislature or executive order of the governor.[7] The states were undoubtedly also impelled by their desire to share in the public
works funds and recovery programs (federal approval of public
works projects required prior clearance by a state planning
agency).[8]

Aside from public works programming, the activities of the
state planning boards during the 1930's centered on surveys and
research, planning assistance to localities, and consultations with
operating departments of the government. While the actual
activities were quite modest, the general approach and the
reports tended to stress comprehensiveness in planning. No particular problem or activity focus for the planning emerged. As
public works planning and construction lost its momentum
toward the end of the 1930's, the state planning network fostered
by the federal government began to evaporate. States increasingly
merged their planning boards with "development" agencies or

[7] Two multistate regional planning agencies—the New England Regional
Planning Commission and the Pacific Northwest Regional Planning Commission—were also established in this period.

[8] The enthusiasm for state planning within the states was bipartisan. For
example, at a meeting of the Kansas State Planning Board in January 1935,
Governor Alfred Landon pointed out that "the State Planning Board being
in close touch with Federal and State Departments can perform effective services for both especially in coordinating the varied phases of the relief program." National Resources Board, *State Planning*, p. 12. In spite of the
enthusiasm, the states contributed relatively little to supporting the state
planning programs. During the five year period 1934-39 the states covered
only one fifth of the total of $11,500,000 spent for state planning purposes.
"The degree of dependence upon the Federal Government is shown by the
fact that at the end of 1937, 82 per cent of the employees of the state planning
boards were furnished by the Works Progress Administration. . . ." Albert
Lepawsky, *op. cit.*, pp. 14-15.

transferred their functions to various departments of the government.[9]

A truly significant development in regional planning came into being with the creation of the Tennessee Valley Authority in 1933. TVA planning evolved directly from the agency's basin-wide operations, which included water control, power development, development of water transportation, afforestation and soil erosion control, and fertilizer production; also (particularly in the 1930's) agricultural and industrial development and local community development. It is interesting to note that the general (nonoperational) planning activities, which even at their peak in the early period were not very extensive, diminished over the years.[10]

[9] This was foreshadowed as early as 1935 when New Hampshire merged its two-year-old planning board with the ten-year-old state development commission. The Kentucky planning board was abolished in 1936, and the planning agencies of Connecticut and Maine were abolished the following year; by the end of 1939, nine additional boards had been merged with other agencies or were abolished entirely.

"In retrospect, many students and practitioners of government consider that the educational effects of the planning boards of the 'thirties had more far-reaching significance than any concrete piece of work. The boards contributed much to a greater recognition of the need for the orderly development of state resources and for the joint consideration of programs by the different affected agencies and groups." Council of State Governments, *Planning Services for State Government* (Chicago: Council of State Governments, 1956), p. 23.

[10] In 1935 a National Resources Committee report described TVA planning as follows: "Charged by Executive order of the President, issued in pursuance of the TVA Act, with the duty of making surveys and plans for the general purpose of 'fostering an orderly and proper physical, economic, and social development' in the region, the TVA has assumed a planning function which is not isolated, but rather inextricably tied up with developmental powers. It has thus become more than a 'regional planning' agency; it is a 'regional development' agency. Soil-erosion control, for example, is not only being planned but is being earnestly and vigorously implemented. A water-control program is being planned and executed. . . . Indeed, so much attention has been given by the TVA to tangible results that the broad planning function has suffered somewhat." National Resources Committee, *Regional Factors in National Planning* (Washington, D.C., December 1935), pp. 83, 85.

Roscoe C. Martin, in summing up two decades of TVA experience, makes the following comments: "There were those in the beginning who expected the TVA to assume active leadership in regional planning. . . . The Board did proceed initially along lines suggested by the directive [authorizing broad

Regional planning as related to operating activities assumed some importance also in the case of a number of the federal agencies. The National Resources Committee, in its report on *Regional Factors in National Planning* (1935), described the work of fifteen bureaus which were using "definitely demarcated regions" for the purposes of planning and program making.[11] Within the states, examples of regional planning connected with departmental operations appeared here and there in the 1930's, e.g., in relation to land planning in Michigan and Wisconsin and water planning in California.

Metropolitan and county planning expanded tremendously in the 1930's under the general stimulus of the widespread interest in planning and under the specific stimulus of federal (and some state) assistance. The number of county and metropolitan plan-

---

regional planning], establishing a division which emphasized regional planning and giving considerable attention to such subjects as land and water use planning. After 1937–38, however, gradual modification of the early planning orientation set in. The regional planning unit was eliminated, some of its functions being dropped entirely, others being shifted to other divisions; and the regional planning emphasis which the law seemed to contemplate went into limbo. In place of concerted action in regional planning by TVA, there developed the by now familiar pattern of agreements with the cognate agencies of existing governments—with state departments of conservation and forestry, for example, and with state and local planning bodies. Thus has primary responsibility for planning passed from the *TVA* to state and local agencies, with the former remaining active chiefly in the role of encourager, adviser, and technical consultant." TVA: *The First Twenty Years,* edited by Roscoe C. Martin (University of Alabama Press and University of Tennessee Press, 1956), p. 265.

[11] Most of these bureaus were in the Department of Agriculture and the War Department, including the Forest Service, Extension Service, Bureau of Public Roads, and the Corps of Engineers. For example: "The Forest Service of the Department of Agriculture plans regionally for the protection, development, and administration of forest, range, and wild lands." "The Bureau of Public Roads plans regionally for the construction of roads in national forests and national parks." Land use and agricultural planning were carried out by a number of local groups established specifically for that purpose. These included the County Land-Use Planning Committees and the Community Committees working with them, the District Soil Conservation Committees, the Local Committees of the Agricultural Adjustment Administration, and the Local Grazing Advisory Boards of the Forest Service. National Resources Committee, *Regional Factors in National Planning* (Washington, D.C., December 1935), pp. 75, 76.

ning agencies increased from 85 in 1933 to 506 in 1936 (316 of which had official status).[12] However, very few of these agencies had any staff facilities for active planning work. Some of the private (nonofficial) regional planning organizations had a fairly influential role in the planning for their areas, but neither these organizations nor the official regional and county agencies represented an effective solution to the problem of integrating city and regional (metropolitan) planning.[13]

THE POSTWAR PERIOD—THE "AREA-DEVELOPMENT" PUSH

By the time the National Resources Planning Board was abolished in 1943, state planning through a central staff agency had for some years been subject to a process of attrition—characterized by the failure of state governments to appropriate funds for planning or to re-enact state planning legislation. This process was accelerated during the war years, and by the end of World War II more than thirty of the former state planning boards no longer existed in their original form. However, during the war period, postwar planning and readjustment agencies were authorized in almost half the states (mainly to promote postwar re-employment) and at the same time a number of combined state planning-and-development agencies were established. When the postwar recession which many expected did not materialize, the special planning agencies went out of existence and in most instances permanent planning or planning-and-development agencies took over the functions of the "postwar" units. Increasingly "development" pushed "planning" into the background. The state governments ". . . thus returned, with full vigor, to the nineteenth century idea of economic development, although with a somewhat new emphasis. A new organizational pattern had emerged." [14]

12 National Resources Committee, *Status of City and County Planning in the United States* (Washington, D.C., May 15, 1937).

13 See Robert A. Walker, *The Planning Function in Urban Government* (Chicago: University of Chicago Press, revised edition, 1950), pp. 122–28.

14 Council of State Governments, *Planning Services for State Government* (Chicago: Council of State Governments, 1956), p. 27. As compared to the nineteenth century efforts in the field of economic development, the present effort emphasizes industrial development rather than transportation or agri-

The state governments have moved almost en masse to economic development and promotional efforts—more or less in the same "group" fashion as they had embarked upon central state planning in the early 1930's. In most instances the shift has taken place without any serious effort being made toward resolving the question of the appropriate relationship between state planning and state development activities.[15]

Currently, forty-six of the states have official economic development agencies and, in addition, fifteen of the states have, or are about to set up, Development Credit Corporations, providing loans to community groups and industrial borrowers. The state efforts in economic development are strongly bolstered by the activities of many other development-minded groups: local government area-development agencies; local and state chambers of commerce; railroads, banks, private utility companies, and other private business groups; interstate regional agencies (such as the New England Council); and several agencies of the federal government, particularly the Office of Area Development of the Department of Commerce. In its issue of October 1956, *Industrial Development,* The National Magazine of Area Analysis and Business Site Selection, points to the startling fact that there are now more than 5,000 area-development groups in the country. "On the average, two new groups come into existence every week." [16]

---

cultural development, there is little if any consideration of the question of state-owned enterprises, and there is at least some connection to planning. Lepawsky, *op. cit.,* pp. 19 ff.

[15] There have been some exceptions. Maryland, for example, set up a commission to study the future of planning in the state. The Commission on State Programs, Organization and Finance, *Improving State Planning in Maryland* (November 1956). Pennsylvania, Tennessee, and a few other states have also given serious study to the problems of organizing appropriately both planning and development activities.

[16] ". . . The services offered cover a wide range in both scope and quality. Hundreds of development units are staffed with full-time development specialists capable of rendering professional services. In many cities you may call upon a development 'team' which includes highly qualified experts covering every aspect of plant location. In fact, there appears to be a very definite trend toward a more professional and a more scientific approach to development programs." *Industrial Development,* October 1956, p. 45. A useful description of the present state of area development activities is provided by Victor

Out of this snowballing area-development movement has come a strong demand for persons with a number of different kinds of specialized skills, as well as for persons with broad knowledge relating to problems of economic development. Even more pressing has been the resulting search for more knowledge and improved research methodology in a number of fields, such as industrial location and market analysis, together with knowledge concerning the basic forces underlying regional economic development.

PLANNING AND SERVICES FOR THE
BROAD METROPOLITAN REGION

Since the end of World War II the development of regional and state planning has been profoundly influenced by metropolitan urban expansion.[17]

The growth of continuous urban strips, "scatteration," and other urban phenomena (some of which are as yet so "unstructured" that they cannot adequately be described) are presenting new problems and uncertainties for both private and governmental decision makers. Business and government operations are greatly affected by changes in the economic foundations of an interdependent region. The labor supply area, the natural re-

Roterus, Director, Office of Area Development of the U.S. Department of Commerce in "Area Development in the United States—Its Status and Frontiers," address before the Third Annual Western Area Development Conference, October 31, 1956 (mimeographed). In his address, Mr. Roterus stressed the need for technically trained persons as area-development specialists.

17 The statistics on this point are impressive: By 1950, over half of the total population of the country and three-quarters of the urban population was concentrated in the 168 standard metropolitan areas, as designated by the U.S. Census. In that year, 41.5 per cent of the metropolitan population lived *outside* the central city boundaries. Between 1950 and 1955 almost all of the increase in population was in the standard metropolitan areas—11,500,000 out of the total U.S. population increase of 11,800,000. The rural population outside the standard metropolitan areas declined during that period. U.S. Department of Commerce, Bureau of the Census, *Current Population Reports* (Series P-20, No. 63, "Civilian Population of the United States, by Type of Residence, April 1950 and 1955.") There are currently 96 local governments, on the average, in each of the metropolitan areas.

sources base, the regional market area, the efficiency with which materials can be assembled and goods shipped out, the industrial site requirements, and the attractiveness of the environment for family living, are all matters of direct concern to public groups and private enterprises. As a result, the need for knowledge about the regional economy, public fiscal requirements, and governmental structure, and the need for all kinds of planned action along regional lines, come increasingly to the forefront.

Municipal undertakings of many kinds—even those seemingly concerned directly with the central city, such as urban redevelopment and urban renewal—now compel city governments to face problems of population movement and population distribution within the region and of metropolitan transportation. Thus, many operating programs of the central cities compel attention to problems transcending municipal boundaries. In fact, to an increasing extent government services and facilities are being organized on a metropolitan basis through the authorization of a semi-independent status for the service (usually in the form of metropolitan special districts) in order to get around the problem of multiple governments in a single "problem area." Examples of such special districts are:

Transportation and terminal facilities—e.g., Port of New York Authority

Sewage disposal and water supply—e.g., Metropolitan District Commission of Boston

Airports—e.g., Detroit Metropolitan Aviation Authority

Flood control—e.g., Los Angeles County Flood Control District

Electricity—e.g., Omaha Public Power District

Housing and slum clearance—e.g., Cleveland Metropolitan Housing Authority

The suburban and outlying communities face a whole set of difficult problems arising, in part at least, from the fact that industry, commercial establishments, and residences within a metropolitan region are not evenly distributed as among the local jurisdictions so that service requirements and fiscal capacity can be seriously out of balance.

The response to the need for metropolitan-wide planning has taken a number of forms. City planning agencies in quite a few instances—as in New York, Philadelphia, Detroit, San Francisco, and other cities—have devoted an increasing amount of their efforts to metropolitan problems. The metropolitan special district organizations in some cases have not only prepared metropolitan-wide plans for their own operations, but have made broad studies of value to other regional operations. Finally, all kinds of metropolitan (regional) planning units are being established, at an accelerating pace,[18] and a variety of co-operative arrangements, both official and unofficial, are being worked out, usually aiming at the co-ordination of efforts on the part of local governing bodies with regard to such matters as highways, utilities and facilities, and zoning and subdivision control. In some part at least, the expansion of metropolitan planning has been an outgrowth of the U.S. Housing Act of 1954 which provides for federal grants-in-aid for planning work to official metropolitan planning agencies (also for grants to state planning agencies to be used for metropolitan and regional planning),

[18] Almost every month new metropolitan regional planning organizations come into being. In a single issue of the *Newsletter* (monthly) of the American Society of Planning Officials in 1956, the following items appeared under "Regional Planning Notes":

"A four-county planning agency has been agreed upon in the *Puget Sound*, Washington area by the commissioners of King, Pierce, Snohomish, and Kitsap counties.

"*The Meadowlands Regional Planning Board* in New Jersey has been set up to deal with development problems of the area. Its jurisdiction includes East Rutherford, Carlsbad, Lyndhurst, and North Arlington.

"A *Greater Portland Regional Planning Commission* has been formed with Portland, Maine, and ten other neighboring towns participating. It is the first agency set up under the 1955 Maine enabling law for regional planning. A professional staff is being hired to draw up a co-ordinated plan for regional development.

"Regional planning for the northern part of Summit County, Ohio is the goal of a newly established *Northern Summit County Planning Association*. Included in it are the townships of Macedonia, Northfield Center, Sagamore Hills, Boston, Richfield, Twinsburg, and Hudson and the villages of Hudson, Northfield, Boston Heights, Twinsburg, and Peninsula.

"The new *Middlesex Regional Planning Association* in Connecticut, an unofficial agency, is holding monthly meetings alternating between workshops on specific town problems and panel or speaker sessions on broader problems."

but undoubtedly the pressure of local situations has been the major motivating factor.[19]

Alongside of the metropolitan planning movement there has been an increasing interest in the development of governmental structures and arrangements to cope with the problems arising from the juxtaposition of many, often dissimilar, political units within metropolitan communities. Many approaches have been tried or advocated, particularly: annexation (the absorption of territory by a city), city-county consolidation, city-county separation, transfer and joint handling of functions, metropolitan special districts, and federation.[20]

In spite of what seems to be frustratingly slow progress towards improved metropolitan government and region-wide planning, it is evident that we have entered on an age of governmental experimentation and "constitution making." There is a possibility that within the next generation a new structure of urban government—and metropolitan planning—will have evolved in the United States.

One item is worth noting especially: In many communities the experiments with new intercommunity planning arrangements and the lessons learned through co-operative planning efforts might well point the way towards improved governmental structure. This suggests a potentially significant role for persons performing city and regional planning tasks in the "governmental building" period which seems to lie ahead.

REGIONAL PROGRAMS IN NATURAL RESOURCES DEVELOPMENT AND CONSERVATION

There have been some postwar advances in the natural resources field with important implications for regional planning. Possibly most spectacular is the growth in number and scope of

---

[19] For a description of various types of metropolitan organizations established in the decade after World War II, see *Metropolitan Planning*, A Research Report, City Planning Division, University of Arkansas Publication No. 6 (Fayetteville, December 1955), pp. 4–10.

[20] Interest in the last approach has been much stimulated by the establishment of a federated government in the metropolitan area of Toronto, Canada. A description of many local experiments that have been tried and of the

the soil conservation districts. Today there are some 2,700 soil conservation districts concerned with erosion control and soil and water conservation. Behind the individual farm plans lie a great deal of regional information and at times district-wide and broader land- and water-use and agricultural plans. To be effective, this type of planning must include detailed consideration of the important exogenous or "off-the-farm" forces influencing land use and farm operations; and among the most important of these forces are those related to urban expansion, affecting as they do rural land values, land uses, and the opportunity for part-time and full-time off-the-farm employment. The extent to which soil conservation and agricultural planning must be based on broader regional considerations is dramatized by the fact, revealed by a recent study of the Soil Conservation Service, that three times as much arable land is annually removed from agriculture by conversion to other uses than is destroyed by erosion.

Developments since the end of World War II have served to emphasize the need for more extensive land-use planning activities by soil conservation districts, state departments of natural resources and agriculture, and similar units, as well as by regional planning organizations. More complete land and water studies and plans are needed not only to help farmers in individual farm planning, but also to guide communities, highway planners, industrialists and industrial development groups, and land developers. Such studies and plans are needed particularly in urban-rural "tension" areas.[21]

---

major approaches advocated is presented in the Council of State Governments, *The States and the Metropolitan Problem* (Chicago: Council of State Governments, 1956). The authors of the report see federation, urban county, and multipurpose special districts as the most promising solutions.

21 Frank W. Suggitt, "Changes in Land Use," presented as part of the Symposium on Land Utilization in the United States at the annual meeting of the Soil Conservation Society of America, Tulsa, Oklahoma, October 17, 1956 (mimeographed). Mr. Suggitt, who is head of the Resource Development Department at Michigan State University, pointed out: "The soil conservation districts and the Service personnel can be key leaders in the development of the necessary land use plans and dedications of land use. . . . They . . . must be encouraged to better understand the basic changes in America's employment and occupance pattern and to better appreciate major regional shifts in population and land use. Armed with this kind of knowledge, local people in local areas must develop plans for the direction of land use changes. These

A noteworthy advance in regional planning, as underlying an interrelated group of federal government activities in natural resources conservation and development, is marked by the post-war establishment and continuing operations of the Field Committees of the Department of the Interior. These committees are made up of regional representatives of the various bureaus of the Interior Department whose function it is to evolve co-ordinated plans and six-year operating programs for each of the respective regions "consistent with the multiple-purpose concept of resource development." [22] The preparation and annual revision of the six-year programs provide a mechanism for joint planning of departmental activities along regional lines, the attachment of priority rankings to program recommendations, and a close linking of planning and budgeting functions within the department. These signify advances in operating procedures of some actual, and great potential, value.

There have been no strikingly new developments since the end of World War II in the field of river basin planning. River basin studies and plans of a more or less "comprehensive" nature continue to be made by the Army Corps of Engineers and the Bureau of Reclamation. Regional economic studies to provide a firmer foundation for development plans have become frequent and more extensive in scope. A few special studies have been made, representing particularly intensive efforts at joint interagency planning. Outstanding among them are the reports of the Arkansas-White-Red Basins Inter-Agency Committee and the New England-New York Inter-Agency Committee. Potentially important recent developments are the expansion of small watershed planning and development, accompanied by the growth of watershed associations; [23] the passage of a federal flood damage

local plans must be integrated with one another into broader area plans which are sufficiently comprehensive that they can give positive guidance to new land use developments." (p. 11.)

[22] In the Missouri River Basin Region, seven bureaus of the Department of the Interior are engaged in this joint planning and programming effort. They are: Geological Survey, Bureau of Land Management, Bureau of Reclamation, Bureau of Mines, Fish and Wildlife Service, National Park Service, and Bureau of Indian Affairs.

[23] Under Public Law 566, adopted by the 1954 session of Congress, local government organizations are responsible for the planning, construction, and

insurance law, with the availability of insurance conditional upon flood plain zoning; and the apparent establishment of flood control as a fully nonreimbursable federal function. In general, it seems clear that regional planning for water development is certain to continue to occupy the attention and energies of a large number of persons in federal, state, and local agencies.

HIGHWAY PLANNING

The extensive programs of highway construction of the past decade, carried out by the federal government, states, localities, and toll road organizations, have involved regional planning—but usually of a quite limited variety. Projections underlying highway construction plans normally should—but not always do—have an underpinning of regional economic projections and economic-impact studies, as well as the usual traffic studies. In recent years several extensive ad hoc transportation studies have been sponsored by public groups, looking to the provision of information—with regard, for example, to such matters as transportation patterns and traffic growth potentialities—which can help in the making of public and private decisions concerning transportation. Outstanding among these are studies of transportation in the Detroit, Philadelphia, and Chicago metropolitan regions.

A great acceleration of highway construction is anticipated under the Federal-Aid Highway Act (Public Law 627) which envisages a thirteen-year program of highway construction, costing some $33.8 billion, highlighted by a 41,000-mile interstate system of superhighways.[24] The ultimate value of this multi-billion-dollar program undoubtedly will depend in no small way on the extent to which it is based on careful regional economic projections and economic-impact studies and on soundly conceived regional plans for urban expansion and economic and

operation of improvement facilities in small watersheds; the states have the responsibility of reviewing and approving plans of local units; and the federal government assists by sharing the costs of construction of improvement facilities.

[24] Ninety per cent of the cost of the Interstate and Defense highway system will be borne by the federal government, and the remaining 10 per cent by the states.

resources development. Quite obviously, the highway program will be one of the crucial leverages in the form and direction future urban expansion will take; it will also greatly influence regional economic growth in most parts of the country. It is no exaggeration to say that never in our national history has a centrally conceived construction program offered such a large opportunity for shaping directions of population and industrial growth. If incipient notions of dispersion, particularly in connection with civil defense, are to be implemented, they would clearly have to be tied to decisions relating to the highway program. Thus, the knowledge, skill, and breadth of outlook of the men who will plan and design this highway system will have much to do with the soundness of future development in many fields. The possibility of improving the quality of highway planning and highway planners deserves immediate attention.

II Characteristics of
the Regional Planning Field

A number of conclusions concerning the nature of the regional planning field can be drawn from the experience to date with regional and state planning and are suggestive for the question of education.

1. *Developments of the postwar period are essentially long range in nature.* One point seems fairly certain: the postwar developments described briefly above are neither temporary nor trivial. They signify what might be characterized as a conscious and serious effort on the part of the U.S. society to provide for group adjustment to the consequences of the advanced industrial revolution (or, more accurately, the industrial-services revolution) —that is, adjustment to an age of rapid urbanization and almost ubiquitous urban culture, of expansion in manufacturing and services and of increasing industrial automation, of scientific and

highly productive farming, and of a high general level of living.

The country has come increasingly to realize that agriculture cannot absorb more workers, that all of the growth in the population and labor force must be absorbed by manufacturing and service activities, and that most of these activities are likely to cluster about the urban industrial centers of the nation. Under the circumstances, a growing interest in industrial and service development and metropolitan expansion in every part of the country is hardly surprising.

Several features seem to be emerging. One is increasing concern with the questions of achieving *both* economic objectives (opportunities for better jobs, more profits, high productivity) *and* "social" objectives (mainly good family living conditions). The result is, at one and the same time, strong pressure for "area development" efforts to help bolster the economic future of the local community (as well as the nation), and pressure for more and better public services, for provision of open space and recreation facilities, and in general for the maintenance or creation of a good environment for family living. Thus, the community increasingly becomes an important basis for organization. That is, our society has come to put high priority on objectives calling for many activities dependent on community organization. And it becomes more and more evident that community organization for planning and action must evolve inherent flexibility and relative efficiency not too far short of the level characteristic of the private corporation—long the key organizational form for achieving a host of group objectives in this country. Questions touching on the quality of city planning and regional planning, and improvements therein, are basically concerned with this issue.

New arrangements for coping with problems of widespread urbanization, industrialization, and service growth are being put together in the same pragmatic manner in which the nation earlier developed institutions to advance group interests in farming (such as the homesteading provisions, agricultural experiment stations, extension services, land grant colleges, and the farm subsidies). The state planning and development agencies, the public and private area-development groups, the voluntary metropolitan (regional) planning organizations, and the other new institutions are clearly in their rather primitive beginnings.

The federal government—following a well-established pattern—has begun to extend financial aid to states and localities to help out with their urban problems, including funds for city and regional planning. Federal highway aids and financial assistance for natural resources conservation and development are more extensive than ever. Federal assistance to promote economic growth, and particularly industrial development, in relatively depressed regions seems to be on its way. There is every reason to believe that the grant in aid—that great invention for overcoming some of the difficulties of a federal system—will be employed in increasing volume.

In general, then, it seems likely that the growing pressures on the local, state, and federal governments to face up to some of the difficult group problems stemming from the advanced industrial revolution will result in continuing expansion of regional planning and development activities, as well as of city planning and related activities.

2. *Experience to date suggests that regional planning in the United States has its best opportunity for substantial and continuous contribution when it is tied to ongoing, clearly focused operations. There is an important difference, however, as to whether such planning is narrowly or broadly conceived.* Planning in the United States has consistently received maximum support where it has been directly concerned with quite concrete —and troublesome—problems for which specific operating programs have been evolved. This helps to explain why city planning (which has generally dealt with the more pressing urban problems and which has had, understood and accepted core concern with physical development) has received substantial support. It suggests, also, that the history of the state planning agencies has not been accidental but has followed a rather predictable pattern—the turning to a new set of relatively specific problems (those of area development) once their earlier concrete task (of planning for federally supported public works construction) disappeared. In the federal government, also, planning geared to specific operating tasks, and to related problems of policy formulation, has had the most consistent support. This has been true in the case of the operationally oriented planning of the TVA as well as of the Army Corps of Engineers and the Bureau of Recla-

mation. It is true also of military planning, monetary and fiscal planning by various agencies including the Council of Economic Advisers and the Treasury Department, and a number of other activities.

At the same time, it seems evident that it is not enough merely to point out that planning tied directly to operating programs can normally get support (while central "comprehensive" planning cannot.) [25] In all too many cases operating programs are planned in an isolated fashion without serious consideration of other, and even closely related, activities or of social objectives which transcend those of the specific operating program. There is always the danger that an isolated program can do as much harm as good (as an "upstream" development program which seriously damages "downstream" interests). Or in less extreme cases, an isolated operating program can fall far short of achieving its optimum contribution to a total situation—say, in the case of a highway program, to orderly and sensible metropolitan urban expansion.

What seems to emerge for the immediate future is the possibility of significant improvement from the working out of *strategic linkages* (or linked programs) which can serve as the focal points of government planning activities. This would happen, for example, if a state government were to seek to plan in a joint fashion for the various activities impinging directly on its economic (or area) development effort. In that case, it would see quickly the connecting links between its area-development work, its aid to local community planning (creating a community environment attractive to both industry and workers), its natural resource development work, its highway programming, and other

[25] It seems evident now that the National Resources Planning Board notions of general comprehensive central planning at every level of government—as presented in the Board's various publications and over-all approach—have had no sustained basis of popular or political support in the United States. One can think of any number of reasons why this is so. It is possible to point to the fact that these notions do not fit the strong pragmatic element in American culture, economics, and politics [on this question, see the interesting discussion by Daniel J. Boorstin, *The Genius of American Politics* (Chicago: University of Chicago Press, 1953)]; that they do not fit the bias in favor of decentralized decision making; that they do not fit the complexities of a "loose" federal system.

related activities. "Strategic planning" of this type—broadly directed at a whole group of interrelated activities—could be expected to highlight the fact that the economic development problem is not one of merely attracting industry but of creating an environment conducive to "optimum" development of all the productive resources and activities: agriculture, industry, commerce, and services. It would also be certain to establish the link between economic development, on one side, and, on the other, the creation of better living conditions in communities and attractive standards of public services and facilities throughout the state. In the same fashion, programs aiming at water conservation and development would not be treated in an isolated fashion (as is so often the case today), but would be directly linked by way of estimates of water requirements for projected industry and population.

A prime example of the type of relatively effective planning that can emerge from such "strategic" planning, centering mainly on economic development and an improved community environment, is provided by Puerto Rico.[26]

It is interesting to note—but not surprising—that the major activities that seem logically linked together are precisely the ones to which the term "development" is frequently attached; thus, economic development or area development, natural resources development, highway development, and metropolitan urban development (as contrasted with governmental regulatory activities, education and health services, and so on). These are also activities which, in programming, must be treated in terms of essentially unique physical and locational characteristics and patterns (again, as contrasted with most regulatory, education, health and welfare services, to which relatively uniform *state-wide* standards can generally be applied in operations).

Just as these strongly linked activities seem to provide a firm basis for actual joint planning activities, they would also seem to furnish an effective and viable basis for education and research programs centering on regional planning and development. Persons concerned with these closely related regional planning and development activities, when brought together in a training

[26] See the author's *Puerto Rico's Economic Future* (Chicago: University of Chicago Press, 1950).

program, can not only learn from each other but can come to see the points at which their activities interlock.[27]

Many other types of improvements are needed, of course, to overcome the present inadequacies in regional planning. Among the most important are improvements in planning the operations of government agencies, including better program planning as well as more effective central (overhead) staff planning within state governments.[28]

All of these are issues for what might be thought of as the middle-range future, the next ten to twenty years—issues which are likely to play a lively role in both planning practice and planning education. Projection of the "feasible" or anticipated development of the regional field is, of course, important in analyzing the requirements of a regional training program. But beyond are more general questions concerning the most desirable forms that regional planning might take to achieve optimum effectiveness. These questions deserve attention at the research level.

3. *A distinction needs to be made between city planning and regional planning as fields of knowledge and skill, because each deals with different sets of substantive problems.* In a country whose working population is employed mostly in agriculture and other extractive activities and whose cities are relatively small and compact urban communities, the distinctions between city (or urban) planning and regional planning would come out rather clearly. Regional planning would tend to be concerned with resources development and possibly with programs of economic (mainly agricultural) development; city planning, with

[27] The various groups that can be brought together in a regional training program are discussed later.

[28] A highly suggestive treatment of the form such central staff planning might take is provided in a report prepared by the Council of State Governments, *Planning Services for State Government: A Summary of the Need and Suggestions for Organization* (Chicago: The Council of State Governments, 1956). See also *A Model State and Regional Planning Law,* recommended by the National Municipal League in 1954. A specific recommendation for central staff planning in the State of Maryland, following in the main the pattern suggested by these two reports, has been presented by The Commission on State Programs, Organization and Finance, *Improving State Planning in Maryland* (November 1956).

improvements in the physical environment of the closely knit urban communities. However, when extensive urban-industrial centers become the dominant force in almost every aspect of national life, the distinctions become harder to make. The urban centers themselves must logically be conceived in regional terms— actually the most significant type of region for many kinds of private and governmental activities. Urban-type developments spill out into the countryside, and the watershed or farming region is no longer chiefly a "resources region." Finally, by the very pressure of the problems, every level of government becomes involved in urban matters, in resources matters, and in economic-development matters, and city planning can no longer be treated as synonymous with local planning nor regional planning as a function solely of the state and federal government.

In spite of all these complications and interrelations, it is possible to distinguish between two sets of substantive problems (and the knowledge and skills involved in dealing with them). These are necessarily conceptual distinctions; in reality, there is substantial common ground and many interconnections. The first group are the *problems of the urban environment* within the city and within the metropolitan region; the other group are the *economic and resource development problems* of the "resources region," the metropolitan region, and other types of regions and significant areal designations (such as the state and county).

The first set, or "cluster," of problems stems mainly from a concentration of population and the need for accommodating many diverse functions in a limited space. These are the problems characterized by many contacts and interdependence caused by high-density human settlement, with all sorts of physical and land-use concomitants. They are the central concern of the city planner, although he may well have other tasks as well. Among the problems in his "focal" concern are those of mass transportation, traffic and parking; compatibility of urban land uses; provisions of adequate urban facilities; neighborhood and structural soundness, including slum clearance and urban renewal; open space for recreation of the city folk and for other urban purposes; and many other problems related to what might be called the logistics of large numbers and high density. (Even "exurbia" has high density compared with nonurban communities.) Spatial and land-use planning are a central urban planning focus, since a key objective of the planning is to arrange that space be used in such a way that the many different urban functions and activi- ties can be carried out with a minimum of cost in money, time, and inconvenience.

The other problem "cluster"—that of economic and resources development within metropolitan regions as well as within other kinds of regions—requires planning which, when broadly con- ceived, is concerned with the development—by private enterprise, public agencies, and mixed arrangements—of agriculture, indus- tries, services, and other economic activities of the region, of natu- ral resources, of transportation and communications, and of urban centers. When effectively organized, such planning should relate regional considerations to a still larger framework; thus, it would look at the question of the healthy economic growth of a given region within the context of over-all national economic growth, and of the development of a region's resources within the context of the evolving national, as well as regional, resources demand and supply situation. Urban communities figure importantly in this type of planning, but they are dealt with chiefly as centers of economic activities (for example, as sites for industries), as the cores of transportation and communication networks, and as the nodal points of all sorts of transfers and flows. Communities as places of family living are an important concern, but major re- liance for dealing with this matter would logically be placed on city planning and associated activities. In an important sense, regional planning is concerned with the physical-economic frame- work for city planning.

Certain elements are conceptually central to regional planning and, even where they do not directly influence developmental practices, do tend to influence goals and planning standards. An example is the emphasis on the importance of the natural environ- ment, on certain "unities" in nature, and on the co-ordinated development of natural resources where this is appropriate.[29]

___

[29] The principle of the multiple-purpose planning and development of a river basin, with full regard for upstream and downstream considerations and for recreation and wildlife as well as hydroelectric power and water transpor- tation, serves to symbolize this point. Concern with the effects on water supply and on flood conditions of certain types of suburban and "exurban" develop-

Another example is the stress on the interrelatedness of the various elements of the economic fabric (or the "unities" in economics), so that attention is directed—or should be—to all the strategically important requirements for healthy economic growth of a region, including the social overhead items (transportation, utilities, public services) and on the less obvious economic opportunities, as in recreation and tourism and in agricultural specialties.[30] And, of course, there is a continuing concern with the appropriate area (region) for various planning problems and types of activities; that is, the geographic area whose physical and man-made features and interdependent elements provide an appropriate focus for the planning. Thus, for example, a number of different regional demarcations might be employed in coping with the various problems of what is normally called *a* metropolitan region: the urbanized area, the watershed, the commuting region, and the local market area. When sensibly handled, regional planning is capable of dealing with complex areal demarcations, if necessary in solving problems, and does not concern itself with neat regional demarcations which lend themselves to easy mapping.

It is important to note that in the United States today, *every* level of government tends to be concerned with *both* of these problems and activity clusters. Thus, not only do we find that urban (or city) planning is being carried out by cities and by metropolitan ("regional") planning organizations of many types, but we also find that the states and the federal government are involved in urban planning through financial and technical assistance to local and metropolitan agencies. The state and federal activities, no less than the local planning activities, call for urban planning ability of a high order.

On the other side, a number of the city and metropolitan planning agencies have devoted serious attention to questions of economic (or area) development and resources development on a

---

ments in metropolitan regions is also suggestive of this central element in regional planning.

[30] The lessons some of the industrial promotion groups are beginning to learn about all the various elements which come into play in establishing an environment conducive to industrial expansion within an area have long been central to the concept of regional planning.

broad region-wide basis. These agencies are concerned with such matters as watershed development and water supply from distant points; open spaces, forests and parks for outdoor recreation; interurban transportation; and industrial development, i.e., attracting industries to the community. In other words, local and metropolitan agencies (as well as state, interstate, regional, and federal agencies) tend to be involved in planning activities relating to regional economic and resources development.

The fact that every level of government should be concerned with both groups of problems is not surprising (although it is not as widely recognized as it might be). In our federal system it is to be expected that internal matters that are of urgent concern to many people—and therefore usually of political importance—will quite often involve all governmental levels in one way or another.

What this suggests is that each level of government employs— or is likely to employ in the future—persons with special knowledge and skill in both "clusters."

4. *Many types of nonplanning activities are related to the two "problem clusters" and these involve knowledge and skills similar in many respects to those needed for the planning tasks.* Both problem clusters involve many activities other than those of planning. Thus, the urban-environment cluster includes many private and public activities of a nonplanning character, such as real estate promotions, municipal government operations of various types, and housing-construction research, to mention only a few. All these call for knowledge of the urban environment and skills which are often closely related to the knowledge and skills needed for urban (or city) planning. In the same way, there are many nonplanning activities intimately related to the problems of regional economic and resources development that require knowledge and skills not far removed from those involved in regional planning (as set forth in this paper). Many of these nonplanning activities are of a research or a promotional nature. These relations can be graphically presented by simplifying and abstracting the complex real situation.

Within the larger regional cluster one of the main types of activities and skills which has recently come to the fore is that of "area" research and the provision of information touching on

TWO PROBLEM CLUSTERS

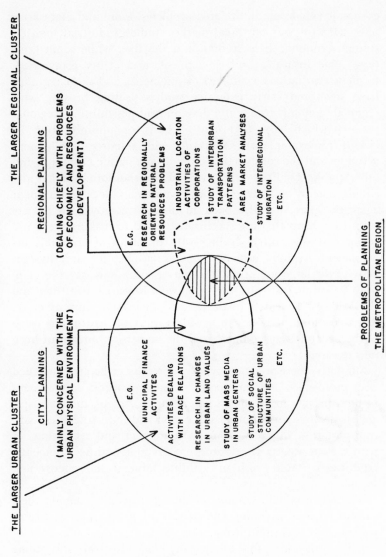

THE LARGER REGIONAL CLUSTER

REGIONAL PLANNING

(DEALING CHIEFLY WITH PROBLEMS OF ECONOMIC AND RESOURCES DEVELOPMENT)

E.G.

RESEARCH IN REGIONALLY ORIENTED NATURAL RESOURCES PROBLEMS

INDUSTRIAL LOCATION ACTIVITIES OF CORPORATIONS

STUDY OF INTERURBAN TRANSPORTATION PATTERNS

AREA MARKET ANALYSES

STUDY OF INTERREGIONAL MIGRATION

ETC.

THE LARGER URBAN CLUSTER

CITY PLANNING

(MAINLY CONCERNED WITH THE URBAN PHYSICAL ENVIRONMENT)

E.G.

MUNICIPAL FINANCE ACTIVITES

ACTIVITIES DEALING WITH RACE RELATIONS

RESEARCH IN CHANGES IN URBAN LAND VALUES

STUDY OF MASS MEDIA IN URBAN CENTERS

STUDY OF SOCIAL STRUCTURE OF URBAN COMMUNITIES

ETC.

PROBLEMS OF PLANNING

THE METROPOLITAN REGION

(INVOLVING BOTH URBAN AND ECONOMIC-AND-RESOURCE-DEVELOPMENT PROBLEMS) economic expansion and related problems. More and more firms have staffs to carry out areal market studies, industrial location studies, economic base studies, and the like, while some firms (e.g., some insurance, oil, investment, and utility companies), business associations, chambers of commerce, and similar groups have sponsored fairly extensive studies dealing broadly with regional economic trends and development possibilities. Regional research which helps to provide a basis for administrative decisions—for example, in connection with resource development activities and the construction of highways, public buildings, and other public facilities—is carried out or sponsored on a quite sizable scale by many federal, state, county, and local government agencies. There has also been an impressive growth in private consulting firms that are specifically geared to making areal and regional studies, often dealing with problems of economic development. Regional economic studies have become an important activity for large nonprofit research organizations like the Stanford Research Institute, the Southwest Research Institute, and the Midwest Research Institute. And there are many other regional research activities in a wide variety of institutions (such as the Federal Reserve Banks and the university bureaus of business research).

Similarly, there are many types of specialists who are concerned with problems of regional economic and resources development in both private firms and public agencies. Among these are specialists dealing with industrial location and industrial sites, with transportation in every form, with tourism and recreation, or with various aspects of resources conservation and development—land, water, forestry, fish and wildlife, minerals and energy, and so on.

There is a certain amount of interchangeability among these various types of planning and nonplanning activities, and some persons shift back and forth among them.

It is worth noting that today many kinds of private and public organizations employ persons for planning and nonplanning tasks which are clearly regionally oriented, and there are other indications to suggest that there are a substantial number of career outlets (seemingly running into the thousands) for which training in regional economic and resources development would be extremely valuable. The listing in Table 1 suggests the types of organizations concerned with regional planning and nonplanning activities and the types of careers available in the field of regional economic and resources development.

TABLE 1   *Organizations and Careers in Regional Planning and Development: Some Examples*

A. ORGANIZATIONS DIRECTLY CONCERNED WITH
   REGIONAL OR STATE PLANNING

1. *Official City Planning Agencies*
   Examples: City planning commissions of New York City, Chicago, Philadelphia, Los Angeles, San Francisco, Cleveland, Detroit, etc.
   Employ persons with skills in "area" economic analysis and industrial location analysis, population projections, intercity transportation.

2. *Official Metropolitan Planning Organizations,* advisory to local and county governments
   Examples: Metropolitan Planning Commission of Atlanta, Detroit Metropolitan Regional Planning Commission, Metropolitan Planning Commission of Knoxville and Knox County, Tulsa Metropolitan Area Planning Commission, etc.
   Employ some persons with skills in regional economic analysis, land-use planning, transportation engineering, resources planning.

3. *Voluntary Citizens' Metropolitan Planning Organizations*
   Examples: Chicago Regional Planning Association, New York Regional Plan Association, Inc., St. Louis Metropolitan Plan Association, Inc., etc.
   Employ specialists for various types of regional studies, including economic and population studies.

4. *Metropolitan Special Districts*
   Examples: Detroit Metropolitan Aviation Authority (airports), Los Angeles County Flood Control District, Metropolitan District Commission of Boston (parks, water supply, sewage disposal), Port of New York Authority, etc.
   Employ persons with backgrounds in regional economic analysis, transportation planning, transportation studies, facilities planning.

5. *Rural Special Districts*
   Examples: Soil Conservation Districts, Ohio Conservancy Districts, Grazing Districts.
   Employ persons with knowledge of soil and water conservation, land and agricultural planning.

6. *State Planning and Development Agencies*

   Examples: Alabama State Planning and Industrial Development Board, Kentucky Department of Economic Development, New Jersey Department of Conservation and Economic Development, Tennessee State Planning Commission, etc. (46 in all.)

   Employ persons with skills in regional economic analysis, resources planning, industrial-location and industrial site planning.

7. *State Government Departments and Bureaus*

   Developmental planning activities are to be found in many departments, particularly the better organized state government departments of public works, highways, natural resources (including forest, park, conservation, reclamation, fish and game, agriculture, geology, mines, oil and gas, water pollution control, and land management units), public utilities, public health, education, and commerce.

8. *Official and Semiofficial Interstate Organizations*

   Examples: Ohio River Valley Sanitation Commission, Interstate Commission on the Potomac River Basin, Interstate Commission on the Delaware River Basin, Southern Regional Education Board, Council of State Governments, etc.

   Employ persons with skills in resources planning, regional economic analysis, and specialized knowledge of natural resources.

9. *Federal Regional Authority:* Tennessee Valley Authority

   Employs persons with skills in regional economic analysis, resources planning, land-use planning, transportation planning, etc.

10. *Federal Government Agencies*

    Examples: Army Corps of Engineers, Bureau of Reclamation, Forest Service, National Park Service, Soil Conservation Service, Technical Review Staff of the Department of Interior, Bureau of Public Roads, Office of Area Development, Housing and Home Finance Agency, etc.

    Employ persons with a variety of skills in the regional field, including natural resources planning and development, regional economic analysis, highway planning, land-use planning, etc.

B. OTHER ORGANIZATIONS EMPLOYING PERSONS WITH
   BACKGROUNDS IN REGIONAL PLANNING, REGIONAL RESEARCH,
   AND VARIOUS REGIONAL SPECIALIZATIONS

11. Private area-development agencies

12. Private consulting firms specializing in: general economic research, industrial and industrial location research, transportation studies and planning, resources analysis and planning.

13. Private firms (utilities, railroads, banks, insurance, oil, investment, construction, etc.) employing industrial location and industrial site specialists, transportation and public facilities analysts.

14. Research units of Federal Reserve Banks.

15. Nonprofit research organizations concerned with area studies and regional analysis.

16. Universities: bureaus of business research and other research units doing area studies, planning and community service units, teaching and research in regional subjects.

17. Public and private agencies concerned with providing technical assistance personnel for overseas work (touching on regional economic and resources development).

18. Voluntary citizens interstate regional organizations concerned with economic development (e.g., New England Council).

19. Associations of business groups (e.g., chambers of commerce) and of labor groups.

SOURCES: Information supplied by the Council of Metropolitan Regional Organizations and the American Society of Planning Officials; "Metropolitan Special Districts," Table V, *The Municipal Year Book, 1956* (New York: Engineering News Pub. Co.), pp. 52–55; Association of State Planning and Development Agencies, *Directory*, November 1955; Legislative Reference Service, Library of Congress, *Natural Resources Activity of the Federal Government*, (Public Affairs Bulletin No. 76), January 1950.

III *Educational Requirements*

As already suggested, certain types of planning activities and certain kinds of planning problems are common to both city and regional planning. This is particularly true in the case of planning for the metropolitan region, where the city planner and the regional planner would tend to work side by side, with a substantial amount of spill-over in activities being inevitable—and valuable. Because of this, and because both the city planner and the regional planner are necessarily concerned with common procedural elements in the planning process, certain of the same types of knowledge and skill must be acquired by both. Thus, it would be entirely feasible to develop at universities curricula which encompass training for both types of planning work within a single educational program.

At the same time, it is important to appreciate the fact that the regional planner has a *core* interest (that of regional economic and resources development) which is different from the core interest of the city planner (that of improving the urban physical environment). The regional planner shares his interest with many nonplanners, including regional research workers, a wide variety of specialists (such as resource specialists, transportation specialists, and area-development specialists), regional administrators, and others. This common regional focus—as well as the need for advancing knowledge in this rapidly growing field—provides a firm basis for new regionally oriented education-and-research programs at universities that have the appropriate faculty strength and interest.

CAREER CONSIDERATIONS

Often new training programs are established at universities after a strong demand has developed for a certain type of knowledge and skill, and then, under pressure from harried practitioners and employers, a trade-school type of program is set up. The emphasis is on "practical" training and frequently practitioners are brought in to do the teaching on a part-time basis. Currently, a full head of steam is building up on the part of persons who are concerned with "area development" to recruit and train many more persons for work in this rapidly expanding field. Similarly, fairly strong pressure is developing for additional training programs in connection with overseas work, including the training of individuals who are to deal with industrial and area-development matters. Other pressures center on the expansion of training facilities for transportation (particularly highway) planners.

As is usual in such cases, the conception of training held by the advocates of these new training programs is both highly "practical" and quite limited in breadth. It would be a course much to be applauded if—as is not too often the case—the universities were to respond to a demand for training in relatively new and fast-growing fields by taking the initiative and evolving programs that are broadly conceived (looking to the future and not the past or present needs) and that are as exciting intellectually and as high in quality as they are in ultimate practical value.

Regionally oriented education and research programs could achieve just that by providing training that is broad enough and basic enough to serve the needs of a number of interrelated career facets, rather than the needs of a single field of work. The career facets which might be brought together in a fruitful way are:

1. Regional and state planning
2. Area development
3. Natural resources development and conservation
4. Transportation planning, studies, and administration
5. Location and marketing research
6. Regional research (including "area studies" of various types)
7. Overseas technical assistance work in the regional field

The type of training proposed would fit career needs not only of persons who will work in the regional field in the United States, but also of individuals who will work overseas on problems of regional economic and resources development, either in connection with United States and United Nations technical assistance programs or directly for foreign governments or private business groups. A demand for persons who can function effectively in regional planning and development has been generated by the U.S. Point IV program and the United Nations technical assistance program. Increasingly in recent years the lesser developed countries have been asking for personnel from the United States (as well as from other technically advanced nations) who can help them with the design and execution of regional programs of resources and economic development and who are able to advise on regional aspects of central planning programs. Regional considerations in national plans tend to loom particularly large in development programs that deal with industry, transportation, energy, and water. The TVA idea of integrated water resource development has aroused enthusiasm in the lesser developed countries, and many river basin programs have been undertaken or projected. Personnel with experience in these fields are consequently much sought after. A sizable proportion (possibly in the vicinity of 10 or 15 per cent) of those working with technical assistance programs overseas are involved in planning and developmental tasks for which the type of training outlined here would be extremely valuable.[31]

The main educational purpose of regionally oriented programs would be to provide *supplementary* education for persons from a variety of professions and disciplines who are already working in the regional field or who intend to do so at the completion of their studies. A training program that had to meet the educational needs of a wide variety of careers must necessarily be broad-gauge and comprehend basic theory and methodology. Thus, the results obtained through such a program could be expected to be different from programs designed to train persons specifically and directly for one specialist field—such as area development, or transportation planning, or market research—where the objective is "practical training" for immediate usefulness. This is not to suggest that broad-gauge programs are less useful than more narrowly conceived training programs. Quite

[31] "The growing list of regional programs includes work now under way in Northeast Brazil . . . ; the Cassa per il Mezzogiorno program in Southern Italy . . . ; the development plan for the state (departamento) of Caldas in Colombia which has only 2 per cent of the area but 10 per cent of the country's population; the plan for economic valorization of the Amazon area, which is more than half the size of the entire United States, but with only about 3.5 million people; the Central American Economic Integration Programme of five small nations; and the many valley development projects ranging from the Damodar Valley in India; the Cacau Valley in Colombia; the San Francisco Valley in Brazil; the Jordan Valley in the Middle East; and many others." Stefan H. Robock, "Regional Aspects of Economic Development," *Papers and Proceedings of the Regional Science Association*, Vol. 2, 1956, p. 51. See also Edward A. Ackerman, "TVA in Its Larger Setting," *TVA: The First Twenty Years*, edited by Roscoe C. Martin (University of Alabama Press and The University of Tennessee Press, 1956), pp. 244–56. The "education and training of Americans for public service overseas" is currently the focus of a two-year study by members of the Maxwell Graduate School of Citizenship and Public Affairs. The study is probing the "training gap" resulting from the rapid growth of public service operations abroad.

the contrary. A more general education—as long as there is a clear central focus—is apt to be more valuable because it tends to provide a good foundation not so much for immediate problem solving as for lifetime learning on the job.

The desirability of broadening the education and outlook of specialists is readily agreed to, as is the value of having specialists come into contact with interdisciplinary study. However, it is obvious that interdisciplinary study, no matter how valuable it might be from the standpoint of educational requirements as such, is not *practically* useful unless it can induce individuals to substitute a certain number of broad interdisciplinary courses for an equivalent number of specialized courses within their own profession or discipline. This suggests that the focus of the interdisciplinary study must be a significant theme with ultimate career value. To be successful, a regionally oriented education program must be able to attract a wide group of specialists—such as transportation engineers, foresters, market researchers, and area-development experts—by giving them the feeling that they will be able to do their job more effectively because of such training.

Normally, it is the person who has been at work for some years who most readily sees the value of this type of training. Individuals who, after a long period of specialized work are given broader decision-making responsibilities, will tend to be attracted to an opportunity for additional education and broadening of viewpoint which might enable them better to deal with complex problems involving many physical, economic, social, and political factors.

Such regionally oriented educational programs might at the same time provide specialized training for persons from the broad disciplines.[32] Thus, an economist might take several courses within a regional program as preparation for the writing of a Ph.D. thesis dealing with some aspect of regional economic growth or location theory or interregional trade, or he might take such regional courses if he wished to devote his career to area

[32] This dual role is, of course, not at all unusual. For example, a public finance course might be a specialized course for an economist, but a means of achieving a broadening experience for the political scientist who previously has had little contact with economics.

research or market research or industry studies. In the same way, a political scientist attracted to work in natural resources administration, might take courses in a regional program as being more useful to him than other types of specialized courses available to him.

This "specialization focus" of a regional program is important particularly in relation to regional research. I believe that the success of any regional program will depend in large part on the scope and caliber of the associated research program for the following reasons.

1. Present knowledge in the regional field is too limited in relation to the complex problems with which the field deals to permit a successful program based entirely on the transmission of existing knowledge.
2. Moreover, giving students an opportunity to take part in ongoing research is one of the most effective educational techniques available for a field like the one discussed here.
3. The regional (or area) research aspect is the most common element in the various fields with a regional focus—whether transportation planning, natural resources development and conservation, market studies, or area-development activities. Therefore, it would be logical to provide the greatest possible strength around the common element.
4. And, of course, a good research program is one of the best ways of attracting high-caliber students.

In all, then, the quality of the research program may well "make or break" a regional program in any university.

A CORE CURRICULUM

It is a simple matter in almost any field of study to draw up a long list of courses which would be *helpful* to students training in that field. On the other hand, one of the best ways of advancing and strengthening a field—and at the same time making it possible for students to obtain an adequate training within a reasonable period of time—is for the faculty to concentrate on working out a small number of *core courses and seminars dealing with the basic principles and methods of the field*. Such a limited basic curriculum is particularly important in this case, since most of the students who enter upon a regional program are likely to take it as a "minor" or during a relatively short period of in-service training.

The working out of a core curriculum is a difficult and demanding task in any field; it is especially difficult where the field is in an early stage of development and only a relatively small number of scholars are as yet concerned with evolving principles and methods.[33]

To give some substance to the suggestion for regional oriented education-and-research programs, there is presented here a generalized treatment of the subject matter which would seem to be central to the regional field. It could be expected that students would be provided an opportunity themselves to work through, and come to understand, such subject matter by way of courses, seminars, workshops, research papers, case studies, and other approaches.

The materials outlined below are, of course, mainly illustrative. For one thing, if a limited (supplementary) training program of the type discussed here were undertaken, it would tend to be administered in a variety of ways—through established departments or schools, interdepartmental committees, research institutes, and so on—and the courses given would logically evolve from the faculty and student interest and strength, available or obtainable. Also, the regional field is very young and, at this stage, essentially experimental. Agreement as to what constitutes the theory-and-methods core of the field will be a long time in coming. The core curriculum suggestions that follow are presented as a basis for further discussion.

1. *Theory and Methods in Regional Economic and Resources Development.* Such a course (or courses) would set out a theoretical construct concerned with the key elements in regional economic expansion and of locational (spatial) arrangements within the context of the national economy and society.

Regional developmental planning and other regionally oriented activities and tasks are more concerned with what might be called "community economics" or "regional economics" than with the economics of the firm. This is not to suggest that basic

[33] A field in this stage is also particularly challenging to work in.

economic knowledge does not apply (it does at every point); rather, what is involved is a special kind of focus—in the same sense that "agricultural economics" provides a special focus. Here the chief concern is with the rates and nature of growth of communities and regions within the context of national growth; with the forces behind the location of economic activities and population; with the economic structure of metropolitan regions; with interregional flows of various types; with the estimation of the economic impact on communities and regions of various kinds of activities, developmental programs, and alternative types of urban spread; and with related subjects. In general, the focus is on basic economic and social forces as they play out their roles and produce concrete results *in space*.

A critical problem is, of course, to identify the key elements in regional growth and to trace the interrelations among these elements, particularly in terms of the spatial end result, and to present these within a conceptual scheme which guides analysis and (hopefully) prognosis as well. This is clearly of central theoretical importance and, at the same time, is a key practical concern, since the objective of speeding economic growth—as well as of meeting family, business, and social needs and demands—tends to be at the heart of most types of regionally oriented activities.

We know that the *pattern of economic activities* that exists in a region determines to an important extent the average level of living (real per capita income) within the region and the rate of growth in output and income. Thus, the relative proportion of workers employed in agriculture, manufacturing, and services in the region is significant; even more important is the character of the industries in these categories—that is, the degree to which they are expanding their facilities, becoming more efficient (e.g., through higher capital-labor ratios), and producing goods or services with a relatively high income elasticity of demand. Changes in consumer tastes, changes in technology of production, transportation, distribution, or consumption, and changes in the organization of industries (all of which influence relative prices) tend to influence strongly the regional patterns of economic activities and the end results obtained. The consequences of these changes take specific form in the number of jobs provided within the existing industries in the region, the level of wages paid, and the extent to which the resources of the region come more or less into demand and the region becomes more or less attractive for new and expanding industries.

The changing situation with regard to demand, supply, and relative prices of goods and services, and the interrelated relative prices of *material resources and raw materials,* sets the context within which the natural resources of the various regions can or cannot profitably be developed and used. The specific determinations with regard to the development and use of the natural resources of a region will depend on both the character of the resources (e.g., quality and accessibility) and the extent of the local (regional) demand as against national market demand, since a transportation cost advantage may well be a determining factor in the decision to develop and use a given resource in a given region.

At the same time, the availability of material resources at favorable prices within a region has much to do with an industry's decision to locate in one region rather than in another. The importance of this factor varies with different types of industries, depending on the relative weight of the material input costs in the total cost picture of the industry.

Other factors that affect industry location include the availability and cost of the needed labor force and the distance (in terms of transportation costs) to markets. The *industry location factor—* which is central to regional economic expansion or stagnation— is thus deeply involved with questions of where the markets and labor pools are (i.e., where people live and where existing industries are to be found).

Both as labor force and as consumers, *population* is seen to play a crucial two-way role. Industry comes to where people are, in order to find labor and markets, and workers tend to move in response to better employment and income opportunities. In a period of a tight labor market, where certain skills especially are in short supply, family preferences in terms of environment for living can be an important "lead" factor; that is, the migration of workers and, particularly, skilled workers, can "pull" industry, rather than be a response to industrial shifts.

The extent to which both people and industries locate within a given region is importantly influenced by the relative attractiveness of the *environment for work and living*. Many factors enter into environmental attractiveness (aside from variation in personal preferences), including the nature of the economic and social overhead (utilities, industrial sites, banks and repair shops, schools and parks), climatic and other natural conditions, and relative accessibility to various focal points of activity. Of outstanding importance is the extent and quality of the regional transportation and communications network. Not only does this influence all relative input and output cost factors and the efficiency of operations, but it also affects the character of the social and cultural environment.

Many of the crucial factors touched upon above can be influenced in one way or another, as we have learned from experience, by conscious *group policy and action,* either through public or private auspices, or by a combination of both. The economic and social overhead is in large part the result of group decisions; certain natural resources situations (as in some of the major river basins) call for public or combined public-private planning and action if the resources are to be developed efficiently and with optimum social returns; and industrial-location and migration decisions can be influenced in a variety of ways by public and private organizations. The theoretical construct, if soundly set up, should provide a useful foundation for analyses and discussions of public policy questions which are important to regional economic growth and resources development. It should also provide a foundation for determining what kinds of statistical data and other types of information are likely to be most valuable in the making of private and public decisions touching upon regional matters.

To be done at all well, both planning and many nonplanning activities within the regional field must generally be based on *economic and population projections* (with suitable treatment of probabilities, ranges, uncertainties). Actually, in all too many instances the projections underlying the planning for developmental programs at present are done superficially, if at all. Often elaborate planning superstructures (for highway construction, resources development, and so on) are built on flimsy projections of the evolving economic and demographic situation within the region, and this is precisely where much planning, and the resulting operations, flounder or fall short of achieving the broader social objectives.

Projections are, of course, central to almost any kind of planning (some estimate of the future situation must almost always be made), but for regional development activities the very purpose of the activities normally relates to the speed and nature of the regional growth within the larger national context. Regional growth, for example, largely determines the highway capacity needed and land and water requirements. Underbuilding or overbuilding in relation to population and economic growth within a region both involve losses to society. Economic and population projections also play an important role in many private decisions that center on "area" activities. This is true, for example, in the case of area market studies, industrial location decisions (particularly where the local market and labor force are significant), and all kinds of developmental investment decisions. This suggests that the making of regional economic and population projections might well be a central theme in this part of the core curriculum, and possibly in other parts as well.

Also, it would seem logical that the students be introduced to the most important techniques applicable in regional analysis, by a systematic presentation within the framework of the theoretical considerations.[34] Thus, in the theory course—as well as in individual and group research efforts—the students would come to see how to tailor analytical methods to the problems involved. For example, the use of regional income, product, and balance-of-payments aggregates might be introduced when the concept of economic progress is discussed. In the same way, re-

[34] The purpose of such methodological discussion would be to introduce the students—including those with limited backgrounds in research techniques—to the types of information and analysis that can be made available. Those with decision-making responsibilities could then come to know what can be drawn on, and what kinds of persons are needed to furnish the necessary information. Students who intended to devote their careers to research would, of course, go on to more advanced methodological courses and would learn more about the techniques in the doing of actual research.

gional multiplier and economic-impact analysis, interdependence techniques of analysis, and other techniques could be introduced at the appropriate points.[35]

2. *The Institutional Framework of Regional Economic and Resources Development* (with a stress on Intergovernmental Relations). Such a course, or courses, would set out in a systematic way an analysis of which groups make what kinds of developmental (including investment) decisions within various types of economies and societies. The common elements as well as the variations within and among various decision-making and control systems would be covered, particularly as touching on public-private and intergovernmental relations with regard to developmental matters. The following might be treated:

(a) Determination of the key factors in the legal, political, administrative, social, and traditional context of public and private decisions that influence regional economic and resources develop-

[35] The background materials that might be employed in a course (or courses) of the type outlined here include the following: August Lösch, *The Economics of Location* (New Haven: Yale University Press, 1954); Edgar M. Hoover, *The Location of Economic Activity* (New York: McGraw-Hill, 1948); Colin Clark, *Conditions of Economic Progress* (London: Macmillan, 1951); Heinrich von Thünen, *Der isolierte Staat in Beziehung auf Landwirtschaft und National Ökonomie* (Jena: G. Fischer, 1930); Tord Palander, *Beiträge zur Standortstheorie* (Uppsala: Almqvist & Wiksells Boktryckeri—A.B., 1935); Walter Isard, *Location and Space-Economy* (New York: Wiley and The Technology Press of M.I.T., 1956); Edgar S. Dunn, *The Location of Agricultural Production* (Gainesville: University of Florida Press, 1954); National Resources Planning Board, *Industrial Location and National Resources* (Washington, D.C., 1943); P. Sargant Florence, *Investment, Location, and Size of Plant* (Cambridge, Eng.: University Press, 1948); Edgar M. Hoover and Joseph L. Fisher, "Research in Regional Economic Growth," in *Problems in the Study of Economic Growth* (New York: National Bureau of Economic Research, 1949), pp. 175–250; Alfred Weber, *Über den Standort der Industrien* (1909), English translation by Carl J. Friedrich, *Alfred Weber's Theory of the Location of Industries* (Chicago: University of Chicago Press, 1929); Børge Barfod, *Local Economic Effects of a Large-Scale Industrial Undertaking* (Copenhagen: Einar Munksgaard, 1938; also, London: Oxford University Press); Harold F. Williamson, *The Growth of the American Economy* (New York: Prentice-Hall, 1951, 2nd Ed.); National Bureau of Economic Research, Studies in Income and Wealth, Vol. 16, *Long-Range Economic Projections*, Vol. 18, *Input-Output Analysis*, and Vol. 21, *Regional Income* (Princeton: Princeton University Press, 1954, 1955, and 1957).

ment. A brief tracing of the history of publicly sponsored transportation, resources, and other developmental projects in the United States (possibly as compared with, say, Japan) could be used as a technique for getting at this subject. This would involve an analysis of the extent to which social and cultural elements can be seen to be influential in the types of developmental activities which tend to be undertaken, and in the way they are carried out.

(b) The main elements in a federal system, including: the question of where authority and jurisdiction derive from, urban-rural conflicts (e.g., as revolving around the control of state governmental machinery), strength and weakness of the various levels of government for different kinds of activities (say, water resources development), and financial problems in intergovernmental relations. "Areal division of powers" would be a central theme.

(c) Principles of organization, communications, and administration in the solution of public problems where more than one governmental authority is involved. This would lend itself to treatment through case studies (U.S. and other) which highlighted key principles, for example, with regard to the possibility and relative ease of region-wide planning and development under various forms of intergovernmental co-operation, and under various forms of public-private (partnership) arrangements. There should be a careful analysis of the different devices useful in achieving co-operation among governmental units, e.g., uniform laws, compacts, organization of public officials, national professional organizations, and so on.

A comparative course of this type is useful in getting at basic principles and methods. It would also be more meaningful for persons training for regional work overseas than would a course centered entirely on the specifics of the U.S. situation.

Planners particularly, but many nonplanners as well, need to develop a deep understanding of the structure and processes of both public and private decision making with regard to developmental matters, and a sensitive appreciation of the key elements in intergovernmental relations. This is as essential for effective planning within a metropolitan region as it is for planning a multistate river basin or a multicounty depressed coal-mining region.[36]

Because of the endless ramifications of these highly complex subjects, it might be useful to center a good part of such a course around a single theme. One theme which might effectively lend itself to this type of treatment is that of Cost-Benefit Analysis and Reimbursement by Beneficiaries, treated not in purely project-evaluation terms but as a framework for general analysis of political structure and organization. This theme can be used to "open up" the subject of intergovernmental relations in a rather basic way.

If one were to take an actual or hypothetical development project in a specific region and trace through, even if in a rough fashion, the private and public costs and benefits, he could say some useful things about the following subjects: What are the implications (as far as "who gets" and "who pays" is concerned) of a public body undertaking the project as against development by private interests? What are the differences between the federal government undertaking it as against a state or a locality or through a "partnership" arrangement? What are the results of various types of reimbursement or repayment arrangements?

36 This area of knowledge is one that is equally important for city planners and regional planners, and of course for many other groups who are involved in public service. Complex intergovernmental relations, particularly in developmental programs, are inevitable in a federal system. The lessons learned through co-operative planning arrangements in metropolitan areas, or through the planning of highway or large resources projects, might well point the way to improved governmental structure in many instances. This suggests a potentially important role for the planner, working with others inside and outside of government, in the experimental period that lies ahead—if he is prepared by appropriate training (as well as by capacity) to work effectively in intergovernmental relations.

On the other side, the political scientist, the public administrator, and others who are preparing to go into public service, particularly at the local and state levels, should have an understanding of the issues involved in metropolitan-wide planning and in regional planning in general—where the problems have no regard for governmental boundaries. Given the present experimental atmosphere, generated by the obvious needs of our metropolitan communities, educational institutions have a responsibility to train individuals who are potential "constitution makers" and who are prepared to cope with the governmental problems of mid-twentieth-century urbanism and industrialism.

Given the fact that each level of government is dependent on different kinds of taxes and each kind of tax taps a different economic group or income class, one could estimate in concrete (even if extremely rough) terms how various groups would be influenced.

The project might be, for example, the development of a watershed to bring an increased water supply to an independent suburban town. One could then take a good look at what consolidation with the central city might mean in relation to this and similar projects; who would gain and lose if the state provided the financing; what would be the implications of development through a private company; and so on. This method of analysis would provide students with a firm grasp of some of the real interests that are involved in various ways of handling a problem and some of the important consequences of administration and financing by the different governmental levels. This technique of analysis (or one similar in intent) would clearly have the advantage of cutting through the verbiage and traditional symbols—"grass roots," "centralization," "states rights"—that can obscure the essential elements of the problem of intergovernmental relations.[37]

[37] Background materials on problems of intergovernmental relations include the following: The Commission on Intergovernmental Relations, *A Report to the President for Transmittal to the Congress,* June 1955 (also, *The Impact of Federal Grants-in-Aid on the Structure and Functions of State and Local Governments,* and committee reports on Agriculture, Highways, Natural Resources and Conservation, etc.); Jane Perry Clark, *The Rise of A New Federalism* (New York: Columbia University Press, 1938); William Anderson and Edward W. Weidner, editors, *Intergovernmental Relations Series,* published by University of Minnesota Press and including studies of intergovernmental relations in Minnesota in courts, highways, agriculture, fiscal relations, local governments, etc.; Arthur W. MacMahon, editor, *Federalism: Mature and Emergent* (Garden City: Doubleday & Co., 1955); Charles M. Hardin, *The Politics of Agriculture* (Glencoe, Ill.: The Free Press, 1952); Paul Studenski, *Measurement of Variations in State Economic and Fiscal Capacity* (Washington, D.C.: U.S. Social Security Board [mimeographed], 1943); James W. Fesler, *Area and Administration* (University, Alabama: University of Alabama Press, 1949); F. L. Zimmerman and M. Wendell, *The Interstate Compact Since 1925* (Chicago: Council of State Governments, 1951); Charles McKinley, *Uncle Sam in the Pacific Northwest* (Berkeley and Los Angeles: University of California Press, 1952; Alvin H. Hansen and Harvey S. Perloff, *State and Local Finance in the National Economy* (New York: W. W. Norton, 1944); Victor

3. *Urbanism in Relation to Regional Economic and Resources Development.* Regional developmental planning is necessarily concerned with urbanism. Whether the planning centers on natural resources development, on highway construction, on "area development," or on a related functional field, certain types of urban questions tend to be extremely important. Among these are questions concerning the relation between urban expansion and national and regional economic growth; the economic and functional relations of the city with the outlying areas of the region and of the city with other cities; and the influence of urban (as against nonurban) patterns of living on resource use, on highway travel and other movements, on use of open space, and so on. The concern in regional planning tends to be with the economic, resource-use, and over-all physical expansion patterns, that is, mainly with urbanism "writ large."

Many nonplanning regional activities are equally influenced by urban phenomena. Industrial location decisions, investment decisions of various types, studies of local and regional markets, and the like, are directly concerned with the urban community.

Persons working in the regional field must develop an understanding of urban structure and urban functions and influences; hence, the study of urbanism deserves an important place in a regional curriculum. Such study might be approached in any number of ways. One of the most useful would be through a "workshop" (or practical "laboratory" or case-study treatment). In such a workshop, a specific metropolitan region might be examined in detail by the students. They would jointly work out economic and population projections (employing techniques learned in the theory-and-methods courses), prepare projections of regional land, water, and open space requirements, and examine the implications of alternative approaches to the over-all physical and economic development of the region. Within such a framework specific developmental projects, either under con-

Jones, *Metropolitan Government,* (Chicago: University of Chicago Press, 1942); Norman Wengert, *Natural Resources and the Political Struggle* (Garden City, Doubleday & Co., 1955); Report to the Federal Inter-Agency River Basin Committee, *Proposed Practices for Economic Analysis of River Basin Projects,* prepared by the Subcommittee on Benefits and Costs (Washington, May 1950); United Nations, *Formulation and Economic Appraisal of Development Projects* (Lahore Lectures), 1951.

struction or recommended by official governmental agencies, could be reviewed and evaluated. This would provide a useful opportunity for students to become acquainted with project and program analysis. Similarly, there would be a fruitful framework to examine the city planning work under way and to review alternative strategies—say, with regard to area-development activities and interurban highway construction—which could contribute simultaneously to both urban (particularly, living environment) and regional economic-development objectives. One of the many by-products of such a workshop would be the opportunity for students to learn to handle maps, aerial photographs, and models within a problem setting.[38]

4. *Alternative Approaches to Regional Economic and Resources Development.* Man has struggled with developmental problems for a long period of time, and there is much to be learned from past experience. A faculty-student seminar, based on student papers, could serve as a valuable forum for the discussion of pertinent policy questions.

The case-study papers would contain a description and evaluation of policies and methods that have been tried in various periods and in different parts of the world. Contact with past efforts and with actual problem and decision-making situations, appreciation of what is acceptable and workable within a given

[38] Some useful references are: Lewis Mumford, *Culture of Cities* (New York: Harcourt, Brace & Co., 1938); National Resources Committee. *Our Cities: Their Role in the National Economy* (Washington, D.C., June 1937); Donald Bogue, *The Structure of the Metropolitan Community* (Ann Arbor: University of Michigan, 1950); Bert F. Hoselitz, "The Role of Cities in the Economic Growth of Underdeveloped Countries," *Journal of Political Economy*, Vol. 61 (June 1953), pp. 195–208; articles in the October 1954 and January 1955 issues of *Economic Development and Cultural Change*, Vol. III, No. 1 and 2, on "The Role of Cities in Economic Development and Cultural Change"; John R. P. Friedmann, "The Concept of a Planning Region," and "Locational Aspects of Economic Development," *Land Economics*, Vol. 32 (February 1956 and August 1956); Harlan W. Gilmore, *Transportation and the Growth of Cities* (Glencoe, Illinois: The Free Press, 1953); Arthur Smailes, *The Geography of Towns* (New York: Hutchinson's University Library, 1953), Robert M. Fisher (ed.), *The Metropolis in Modern Life* (Garden City: Doubleday & Co., 1955); Ben W. Lewis, *British Planning and Nationalization* (New York: The Twentieth Century Fund, 1952); Louis Wirth, Selected Papers, *Community Life and Social Policy* (Chicago: University of Chicago Press, 1956), Part 2.

culture and tradition, and stress on objective evaluations—these, as well as the exchange of ideas about policy with persons from many fields, would provide a valuable background for work in applied aspects of regional planning and development.

RELATED TRAINING

An education program along the lines described above belongs at the graduate level. A student entering such a program should have had, ideally, a good general education at the undergraduate level and should have completed certain prerequisites. Both of these requirements pose serious practical problems, particularly because of the variety of backgrounds to be expected of persons taking the regionally oriented training.

Desirable prerequisites are economic theory at the intermediate level, some work in statistics, contact with either physical or economic geography,[39] and some work in administration and political science. For those who intend to devote themselves to research, some advanced mathematical training would be required. In general, there is much to be said for requiring a good foundation for fairly advanced methodological training, thereby encouraging students to enter or re-enter the regional field prepared to use data in expert fashion. A wise practitioner will know when to rely on his intuition and judgment, but he has an additional powerful weapon if he knows how, as well as when, to use data and analytical materials.

The question of prerequisites is always a difficult one, and a good bit of flexibility in administration is normally required. In a situation where many or most of the students are likely to be at the university on an in-service training arrangement, the problem of bringing students to a common-base level of training and competence requires very serious attention.

[39] Work in the regional field calls for a sound background in certain aspects of geography, ecology, and natural resources. Students must bring with them, or acquire during their period of training in a regional program (possibly through a reading course) some understanding of ecological concepts, an acquaintance with principles of climatology, geomorphology, and the geography of natural resources, and an appreciation of the nature of physical-engineering constraints in resources development.

It has been stressed throughout that there are, clearly, many paths to an education for work in the regional field. Some paths would tend to be relatively general in nature; some, more specialized. Some students from the basic social science disciplines might take the regional curriculum as *one* of their "fields of study" or as a "minor." Thus a student taking a graduate degree in economics might take the regional courses and seminars as a field of concentration, in the same way that he might take "agricultural economics" or "public finance" as a field. A person taking a degree in political science in preparation for a career in the public service might take the regional courses as a "minor field," in the same way that he might take "industrial relations" as a minor. A comparable arrangement might be feasible for students taking degrees in geography, sociology, business administration, law, engineering, and other relatively general fields of study. The regionally oriented training, alongside the training in one of the relevant established disciplines or professional fields, would provide students with a good educational foundation for work in the regional field as planners, research workers, and administrators.

Beyond such more or less general training, the regional core curriculum can be joined with more specialized training to provide education in a number of specializations that are important in the regional field. Thus, there can be an extension of the regional core training into a given type of expertise, or career line. The major possibilities would seem to be specializations in the categories discussed earlier, namely:

(a) *Natural Resources Development and Conservation* (Natural Resources Specialist)

  Background in agronomy, forestry, geography, geology, hydrology, engineering, planning, or public administration.

  Additional courses, beyond the regional core, in problems of resources development, agricultural economics, principles of conservation, and so on.

(b) *Transportation* (Transportation Analyst, Transportation Engineer)

  Background in engineering, business administration, planning, geography, or economics.

Additional courses, beyond the regional core, in land, water, air, and pipeline transportation, statistics, market analysis.

(c) *Area Development* (Industrial Analyst, Area-development Specialist, Industrial Agent for Railroad)

Background in business administration, public administration, economics, engineering, planning, or geography.

Additional courses, beyond the regional core, in advanced economic theory, industry, marketing, public utility engineering, communications, etc.

(d) *Area Marketing and Industrial Location Research*

Background in business administration, economics, engineering.

Additional courses, beyond the regional core, in marketing analysis, location analysis, advanced economic theory, statistics, industry, business organization, etc.

(e) *Regional Planning and Development Work Overseas*

Background in one of the social sciences or one of the professional fields.

Additional courses, beyond the regional core, in anthropology, sociology, economic geography, economic theory, industry, public utility engineering, and so on.

In reverse, persons who have been working in a specialized field and come to a university for in-service training, might well want to take basic general courses in addition to the regional core curriculum, rather than any specialized courses. On the whole, given the nature of the regional field, the balance in the regional training program should definitely be on the side of more general education.

IV *Existing Education and Research Programs:*
Some Gaps and Possibilities

A number of universities in the United States currently are sponsoring research programs or courses and seminars touching upon one or several of the elements that have been described as falling within the scope of the regional field. Some of this is extensive enough to suggest an educational and research focus and interest potentially adequate to permit the establishment of strong regionally oriented programs.[40]

STUDIES WITH A REGIONAL FOCUS

There are schools of natural resources, or a substantial number of courses in resource subjects, at several major universities.[41] Similarly, a number of universities have highly developed trans-

[40] The information in this section is based on a detailed survey of education and research activities at U.S. universities in regional studies and regional planning carried out by Resources for the Future, Inc. (Washington, D.C.) as part of its program in Regional Studies. This survey provides a comprehensive picture of the regional topics that are being studied. Tested against the requirements of a rounded regional educational and research program, it suggests the existing "gaps." A report on the survey, organized and edited by the author, is available in mimeographed form.

[41] For example, at the University of Michigan, Michigan State University, Yale University, Stanford University, Ohio State University, Harvard University, the University of Texas, the University of Wyoming, and the University of Colorado. Generally, the courses are given in a number of different departments and schools. Thus, for example, Stanford University has courses and seminars in natural resources within the Department of Biological Sciences, the Department of Geography, the School of Mineral Sciences, the Food Research Institute, the Political Science Department, the School of Law, and the School of Engineering. The University of Michigan has a School of Natural Resources and Yale University has a School of Conservation.

portation programs in schools of engineering, schools of business administration, or departments of geography. Several sociology departments and research institutes are doing work in "population and human ecology" of great significance for the regional field.[42]

A number of universities are offering a series of courses and seminars, or a full program of studies, focusing on "economic development." While some of these have little or no orientation to regions, they normally cover materials of such direct importance for regional studies that they deserve mention here as potential bases for regional training programs.[43] In a few cases, there are courses or seminars dealing directly with problems of regional economic development.[44] Quite extensive programs of research on regional economic problems are under way at a

[42] At the University of Chicago, the University of California, the University of North Carolina, Brown University, the University of Michigan, and several others. The Department of Sociology at Brown University reports that their graduate seminars in population and in community and human ecology have covered the following topics in recent years: Population Aspects of Economic Development, Migration Mobility and Social Organization, Interrelations of Urban and Economic Growth, Human Ecology, Regionalism, Social Science Approaches to Regional Science, The Structure of the Metropolitan Community, and the Impact of Technological Change on Community Structure and Organization. For an excellent summary of significant contributions in "human ecology," see Philip M. Hauser, "Ecological Aspects of Urban Research," *The State of the Social Sciences,* edited by Leonard D. White (Chicago: University of Chicago Press, 1956), pp. 229–54.

[43] An example is Vanderbilt University's Graduate Training Program in Economic Development, "intended for both foreign students from underdeveloped countries and American students seeking careers in the field of economic development." This interdepartmental program offers the following courses: Seminar in Economic Problems and Research, Seminar in Economic Policies, Economic Analysis, Economic History and Economic Growth, National Income Analysis, Monetary Theory and Fiscal Policy, Agriculture in Economic Growth, Capital Formation and Economic Progress. Programs in economic development are also offered at Harvard University, Stanford University, Columbia University, the University of Chicago, Massachusetts Institute of Technology, and several other universities.

[44] Thus, for example, the Economics Department of Northwestern University offers courses in Regional Economic Development and Economics of Transportation and Location; the Economics Department at the University of Colorado has a graduate seminar in Regional Economics; several departments of geography and of economics give courses in location theory and in "area studies."

number of universities, mainly within bureaus of business and economic research, but also in departments of economics, in schools of business administration, and in departments of geography.[45]

Also of regional significance is the work by members of political science departments and of law schools dealing with political, administrative, and legal factors in local, state, interstate, and regional governmental activities, including problems of intergovernmental relations, jurisdiction and functional areas, and decision making in various types of political and administrative arrangements. Historical and socio-cultural studies of various regions in the United States are being carried out in a small number of universities.

Among the most significant of the regionally oriented research is that dealing with metropolitan regions. Recently, several large-scale foundation-supported studies have been organized under the auspices of major universities which are investigating a wide range of economic and political problems in large metropolitan regions, including the New York and St. Louis metropolitan areas. The scope and depth of analysis of these studies is such that new insights into the structure and functioning of metropolitan regions may be anticipated with confidence. Several of the city planning schools are also carrying out research dealing with problems of the metropolitan region, much of it related to

[45] The type of studies carried out can be illustrated by the titles of some of the recent studies published by the Bureau of Business Research of the University of Maryland. *Southern Maryland: A Tobacco Economy; Coal in the Maryland Economy; Baltimore and the H-Bomb; Industrial Dispersal; Regional Income Accounting and Economic Projection; Interindustry Analysis; Consumer Demands and Resources.*

A substantial number of regional studies are being carried out at various universities under the College-Community research program sponsored by the Committee for Economic Development (and financed by grants from the Committee and the Fund for Adult Education). This program is "designed to give faculty and business participants, working together through research and discussion, an improved understanding of the economy of the state, the region, and the nation."

A useful overview of the range of topics with a regional orientation to which research efforts are currently being devoted is provided by the articles in the *Papers and Proceedings of the Regional Science Association*, Vols. 1 and 2 (1955 and 1956), and the footnote references in these articles.

workshop or laboratory courses, and as part of the city planning education programs.

There are a number of highly developed general programs of regional studies. Several of the most extensive are carried out within departments of geography, which tend to use the region as a focal point of analysis. A few colleges are employing the intensive study of the local region (as the metropolitan region of New York by the City College of New York) as a method for focusing interdisciplinary education.

The University of Wisconsin has, since 1943, offered a degree of Master of Science (or Master of Arts) in Regional Planning. This is an interdepartmental effort and operates under a committee including representatives of all the social sciences, the Law School, College of Agriculture, and the College of Engineering. There is an interdisciplinary core seminar and a field research project, but except for that, reliance in the program is on courses and seminars geared to the requirements of the various individual departments. A specially designed regionally oriented core curriculum has not been evolved.

The University of Pennsylvania in 1956 established a "Ph.D. program in Regional Science," under the policy direction of an interdisciplinary committee. The emphasis is on research, on the development of techniques for regional analysis, and on location and spatial theory. While the program has close ties with the Department of Land and City Planning, its emphasis is essentially on "abstract" studies rather than on planning-oriented or problem-oriented studies. The Department of Land and City Planning offers a number of courses which deal with problems of metropolitan regions.

It is evident that accompanying the postwar expansion in many types of regional activities (described earlier), there has been a literal outpouring of regional studies and a marked revival of interest in research focusing on regional subjects, as well as the beginning of some training efforts in the regional field. All this provides a valuable experimental foundation for further progress, particularly in raising the standards and quality of work in regional planning and development.

To the best of my knowledge, no university has yet attempted to achieve, through a single education and research program, all of the various objectives suggested here: (1) in-service training of persons holding responsible decision-making positions dealing with regional problems; (2) supplementary education of persons from various disciplines and professional fields, through a regional core curriculum, of the caliber to attract first-rate individuals into the regional field; and (3) research to provide urgently needed knowledge in the regional field and to serve as a basis for high-level interdisciplinary training. What is called for is *not* the development of a new professional group but the training of a group of professionals—with different backgrounds and career lines—who can serve effectively in public and private efforts centering on regional economic and resources development and regional planning.

POSSIBLE ORGANIZATIONAL ARRANGEMENTS

The review of education and research activities under way at U.S. universities suggests that there are a variety of sources of strength and interest, certain of which might serve as starting points for the development of strong regional programs aimed at achieving the above objectives.

Clearly, also, given these quite different sources of strength, there are any number of ways in which regional programs might be organized. The following are among the most promising organizational possibilities:

1. A regional program might be established within an existing school—such as a school of planning, a school of business administration, a school of public administration, or a school of engineering—if the school has a broad intellectual and organizational scope and if it has well-developed interdepartmental ties, particularly with the social science disciplines.

2. A regional program might be organized through the establishment of a regional research institute, with the institute sponsoring (after it is well under way) a regional core training program, particularly directed at in-service training.

3. A regional program might be organized under the direction of an interdepartmental committee which would sponsor both regional research and a regional core training program. Nor-

mally, it would be logical to wait until the interdisciplinary research activities have "taken hold" and solid relations have been established among the interested scholars before any attempt is made to devise a training program.

4. A regional program might be organized under the sponsorship of an established department, e.g., a department of economics, a department of geography, a department of political science, or a department of sociology—if several members of the department have a long-standing interest in the regional field and are currently engaged in research in regional subjects. It would be important in such a case that the department have strong interdisciplinary ties, so that it could count on the co-operation of other departments. For example, if an economics department undertook such a program, it should have the co-operation of the political science department to the extent of the latter undertaking the development of a specially oriented theoretical course on intergovernmental relations.

5. Finally, a regional program might be organized under the auspices of a strong, long-established program (school, department, etc.) dealing with one of the key elements in the regional field, e.g., under the auspices of a natural resources program, a transportation program, or an economic development program. Thus, for example, one or two of the transportation schools would seem to have the breadth and strength necessary to undertake the sponsorship of a regional program.

While any number of organizational forms are entirely feasible, it seems evident that certain requirements must be met by all of them if the chances for success are to be maximized. For one thing, the "atmosphere" must be conducive to extensive research activities. Additions to knowledge in the field must be a first order of business, and faculty members must have the time and facilities (and encouragement) to do basic as well as applied research. Also, there must be at least one faculty member who can devote himself full time to the regional program. A new and experimental enterprise always requires "nurturing," and there must always be at least one person continuously on the scene to apply energy and imagination to the undertaking. Finally, there must be financing of the program on terms both generous enough and long-term enough to permit the building of a firm foundation and a careful and relatively slow maturing of the enterprise. It is true here, as elsewhere, that if it's worth doing, it is worth doing well; not elaborately, but well.

REGIONAL PLANNING IN PLANNING SCHOOLS

One of the most feasible of the possibilities for the organization of a regional program, it has been noted, is under the auspices of an *existing* school of planning (if it has evolved firm interdisciplinary connections and if it is research oriented), or in conjunction with the establishment of a *new* school of planning which is broadly enough conceived to permit regional studies and city planning to flourish side by side (with, of course, many interconnections).

A note about terms is in order here once again. Several of the existing city planning schools include "regional planning" in their title. But the term "regional" is here used essentially as a synonym for "metropolitan"; more specifically, it refers to what might be described as "metropolitan urban planning"—dealing with the physical environment of the entire urbanized area of the metropolitan region (and not the city alone), and extending out into the now-rural sections that are subject to subdivision pressures. These planning schools are not now centrally concerned with the economic and resources development problems of the metropolitan region and, except peripherally, do not deal with other types of regions.[46]

Thus, concern with the broader regional focus would at the present time amount to a new enterprise for any of the existing schools of planning, even those that are schools (or departments) of "city and regional planning."

A planning school which undertook a regional program might, of course, focus its attention entirely on problems of regional *planning* (i.e., of the broader region) in the same manner that it is now concerned with city and metropolitan planning, and not

---

[46] Two or three of the planning schools provide a course or two on regional resources problems or on economic development, but these usually stem from the special interests of one of the faculty members and such courses tend to be in the category of "electives."

.touch upon the other elements that have been described as potentially part of a regionally oriented program. If this were done, one or both of two safeguards would have to be provided, in view of the fact that at the present time there are practically no *job classifications* for "regional planning" as such. One safeguard would be to gear the educational phase of the program almost entirely to in-service training, with the provision of one-year (or shorter-term) fellowships to persons already holding responsible posts dealing with regional planning. The other would be to limit admission into the regional planning program to persons who had previously acquired training in a field with recognized career outlets, or had acquired skills on the basis of which they could fit into the job classification systems of either public or private organizations. Persons trained in regional planning can be expected ultimately to find good positions in the field, since there are many such positions, even if not so titled, and the field in general is growing rapidly; but the problem of entrance and job classification should be faced realistically.[47]

On the other hand, the planning school might turn out to be the most logical sponsoring organization for a broad, regionally oriented program within a given university whose strength in the regional field is scattered over a large number of departments and schools. A *good* school of city planning offers advantages as the sponsoring unit of a regional program, if it meets all the necessary requirements (particularly if it has the necessary research strength). The faculty of such a school will tend to work easily with persons from a variety of disciplines and professions; it will tend to be concerned with the application as well as the extension of knowledge; and it will tend to be extremely interested in the problems of regional economic and resources development. Thus, the faculty members who devote themselves to the regional program are likely to find themselves in a friendly and stimulating atmosphere.

However, at the present time only a very small proportion of

47 It is possible, of course, that in the future the situation will change and direct career lines will open up for persons specifically trained in regional planning, just as currently many city planning positions are open to individuals trained specifically as city planners. Such a situation cannot now be anticipated. Moreover, even if it should develop, there would still be good reasons to encourage students to have two strings in their training bow.

the existing planning schools have the type of strength needed to sponsor a new regional program. Also, each of the other potential organizational forms within given universities have special advantages of their own which, in special cases, may more than overbalance the advantages offered by the city planning school. Clearly, no a priori judgment can be made. Moreover, since the purpose in these pages is to stimulate discussion concerning the problems of education for regional planning and development, the question of organizational form need not, nor can it, be carried very far.

The establishment of a regional education and research program without question involves a fair amount of risk. Career lines are as yet far from clear and tasks within the field of regional planning and development are very fuzzily defined. For these and other reasons, the design of regional training programs will be far from easy and recruitment of students will require an unusual amount of care. Yet the effort seems very worth while. For it involves nothing less than the attempt to provide persons from a wide variety of fields with concepts and tools useful for coping with some of the more important public and business problems of the advanced industrial revolution, particularly those centering on urbanization, industrialization, and resources development and conservation.

Education & Research

in Planning:

PART III / A Review of the

University of Chicago

Experiment

WITH JOHN R. P. FRIEDMANN*

I *Background of the*
Chicago Planning Program

In the first two parts of this book questions concerning the appropriate bases for the formal education of city planners and re-

* John Friedmann and I jointly wrote the sections describing the University of Chicago experiment in planning education, employing documents and data on the Chicago Planning Program which had been collected by Mr. Friedmann. The introductory section and last two sections of Part III are my own. Mr. Friedmann was the first student to receive a Ph.D. degree in Planning at the University of Chicago. He is now teaching regional planning in Brazil under the auspices of the International Co-operation Administration.

gional planners have been probed. Some attention has also been given to the problems of how needed changes might be brought about. The focus has been on the professional schools that will turn out the great majority of the increasing number of trained men and women that will be needed.

There is a further question that has not been touched upon directly: In addition to providing better professional training for the different kinds of planners, can the existing planning schools —or possibly one or more new experimental centers—contribute importantly to the theory and principles behind *the whole range of planning activities,* i.e., to planning-in-general?

In a complex society subject to rapid changes planning has become an indispensable social instrument. For some time now planning has been important in many types of organized activities—in efforts to guide the physical growth of urban communities, in the development of natural resources within regions, in the evolution of policies and programs to maintain economic stability or to speed economic development within nations, in the management of industrial corporations, in most phases of military operations, and in the operation of public agencies at every level of government.

It is natural for educators interested in planning and social policy to consider whether the various types of planning activities have common elements that call for skills and outlook similar in important respects, and to ask whether the study of these elements makes up a distinguishable field of intellectual endeavor. If the answer is *Yes*—and there is strong evidence for such a view— then it should be possible to advance knowledge and techniques in planning as a whole through a university education and research program which seeks to develop a systematic body of theory or principles underlying every form of planning, as well as to provide practical training in the specialized skills and techniques of city planning and/or regional planning.

It seems worth while to explore some of the leading problems and possibilities of such an approach to planning education. However, a discussion of this broad topic runs the risk of becoming too abstract and generally hard to pin down. In order to give the subject some structure and substance, an actual example is taken as a starting place and continuing reference point. The example referred to is the experiment in planning education and research carried out at the University of Chicago for the years between 1947 and 1956.

The planning school at the University of Chicago was characterized by the following: (1) an emphasis on planning theory, (2) planning education grounded mainly in the social sciences, (3) practical training not only in city planning, but in regional planning and in planning for underdeveloped countries as well, and (4) a strong emphasis on research. In most of these respects the Chicago school was different from other contemporary planning schools in the United States. Nor is there today, despite the recent extension of scope on the part of some of the existing planning schools, any institution centrally concerned with questions of planning theory and problems of planning-in-general.

The fact that the Chicago experiment has been terminated does not detract from its usefulness as an example here. Neither should termination be interpreted as equivalent to failure; too much was learned, too much accomplished, too many intellectual sparks kindled that are still alive, for that.

The financial and administrative circumstances that were the chief reasons for the closing down of the Chicago Planning Program were unique to the particular setting and a detailed recounting has little relevance here. It need only be noted that the decision to dissolve the Planning Program came during a period of general financial retrenchment at the University of Chicago, after departmental budgets throughout the Social Science Division (in which the Planning Program was located) had been reduced "across the board" by 5 per cent each year for a period of five years. At the same time, other interdepartmental committees in the Division were also being subjected to far-reaching plans for reorganization. The Committee on Industrial Relations, for instance, was also abolished; other committees were cut back. In a period of financial crisis difficult decisions about alternatives and priorities had to be made, and the interdepartmental committees were inevitably most vulnerable.

As a participant, I was too close to the whole experiment to attempt a comprehensive post mortem. The evaluations that I shall offer are only those that appear of use in looking ahead.

ORIGINS AND SPONSORSHIP
OF THE CHICAGO PLANNING PROGRAM

The Planning Program at the University of Chicago began in a generally favorable "climate." Interest in planning education came from a number of sources. The University had for some decades before the end of World War II done outstanding work in the study of urban society, its structure, its politics, its culture. Contributions of note had been made by the departments of Sociology, Political Science, and Geography.

Professors Robert F. Park, Ernest W. Burgess, and Louis Wirth had been the pioneers in urban sociology, and the city of Chicago had become their laboratory. Among them, Louis Wirth especially had been an outspoken champion of planning, and he as well as others on the faculty had come to feel that precisely such knowledge as was being developed in the social sciences at the University of Chicago was needed to guide the physical and social development of our cities.

Some of the University political scientists had come to have a very broad interest in public planning as an element in political and administrative processes. Charles E. Merriam, a noted political scientist and for many years a member of the National Resources Planning Board, felt that the various movements and developments which had resulted in planning activities in the United States were politically and in other ways extremely important, and should be reflected in a planning program within the Social Science Division. A number of others in the Division shared Merriam's view that the problems of formulating policies for development, whether within a municipality or within the larger geographic areas, called for processes, organization, and skills that were similar if not identical, and that on this premise students should be trained and research carried out.[1]

1 Leonard D. White, Herman Finer, Floyd W. Reeves, and Herman Prichett, of the Political Science Department, who themselves had made outstanding contributions in clarifying the role of planning in administration and policy formulation, supported the idea of undertaking a program geared to advancing knowledge concerning the potentialities and limitations of the planning process in government. Among other members who contributed their support were anthropologist Robert Redfield, then Dean of the Social Science

Interest in a planning school at the University of Chicago was expressed from outside the University as well. Walter H. Blucher, then executive director of the American Society of Planning Officials, was anxious to see the start of a training program which could produce professional planners with a deep understanding of society and governmental processes along with the necessary design and other professional skills. A number of local architects and planners also strongly favored the establishment of a planning school in Chicago, birthplace of the modern American city planning movement.

Early in 1945 a committee, composed of faculty members of the University of Chicago and representatives of the American Society of Planning Officials and the American Institute of Architects, initiated discussions concerning the establishment of a planning school. The school was originally envisioned as a cooperative effort. Its headquarters would be at the University of Chicago, but it would join on the one hand with the Illinois Institute of Technology, and on the other with the American Society of Planning Officials. As things later worked out, however, the joint arrangements did not materialize.

The committee envisaged an educational program of unusual depth and scope. "The education for planning and for planners," according to a memorandum of the committee, "should be broadly considered as professional education resting upon (1) a foundation of general education, (2) the acquisition of a systematic body of specialized knowledge in those disciplines which have a special contribution to make to planning, (3) a systematic body of theory or philosophy underlying planning, and (4) specialized skills and techniques which have been found relevant, necessary, and sound in the course of empirical practice." [2] Planning had too long been an "appendage to schools of architecture and engineering." The time was ripe for an experiment that would establish planning as an independent educational enterprise grounded *both* in the social science disciplines and in physical design.

Division, Charles Colby, chairman of the Department of Geography, and sociologist William Ogburn.

[2] "Suggestions for the Establishment of an Institute of Planning" (typed manuscript, May 1945), p. 1.

The recommendation that a "program of education and research in planning" be established as an interdepartmental committee within the Social Science Division was approved by the executive committee of the Social Science Division at the end of 1945.

STAFF

The willingness and ability to co-operate of the established social science departments did not obviate the need for a small separate planning staff.

Rexford G. Tugwell, formerly professor of economics at the University of Pennsylvania and at Columbia, and at that time Governor of Puerto Rico, was invited to come to the University of Chicago to head the program. Tugwell had been Undersecretary of Agriculture during the early 1930's and later director of the Resettlement Administration. For a period, too, he had been chairman of the New York City Planning Commission. As Governor of Puerto Rico, he had been instrumental in setting up what was to become one of the most advanced planning organizations in the hemisphere. He saw in the Chicago program an opportunity to advance the concept of planning as an integrating and guiding force in social activities.[3]

Tugwell arrived in 1946. In the fall of that year, an interdisciplinary Committee on Planning was organized within the Division of the Social Sciences and began to give its first courses of instruction. As yet, the Committee was not empowered to offer degrees in planning.

In the early deliberations of the Committee on Planning it became clear that while extensive resources for planning instruction were available in the Division generally, the "core" content of planning would have to be brought together and new materials developed if the field of planning was to be advanced and if sound graduate training in planning was to be provided. It was

3 Rexford G. Tugwell, "The Study of Planning as a Scientific Endeavor," *Fiftieth Annual Report of the Michigan Academy of Science, Arts, and Letters,* 1948, pp. 34–48. Also: *The Place of Planning in Society* (San Juan: Puerto Rico Planning Board, 1954).

necessary to add faculty members who could develop both the theoretical and the practical (or professional) aspects of planning. The first persons to join Tugwell on the planning staff were Melville C. Branch, Jr., and Harvey S. Perloff. Branch, who was appointed associate professor of planning, had had training in architecture and physical planning and had received the first Ph.D. degree in planning, from Harvard University. He had worked with the National Resources Planning Board and had served as director of the Bureau of Urban Research at Princeton University. His main interests lay in the physical aspects of urban planning, in the history of planning, and in planning theory. Perloff joined the staff as an associate professor of the social sciences. His training had been in economics, political science, and administration. He had served as an economist with the Board of Governors of the Federal Reserve System and as a consultant to the government of Puerto Rico in connection with the island's economic development program. He was concerned with questions of budgeting and planning, state and local finance, regional resources development, and the development of economically less advanced countries.

A year later, Edward C. Banfield and Martin Meyerson became members of the planning staff. Banfield had been an official of the U.S. Forest Service and Farm Security Administration. His interests lay in rural land-use planning, the survey of small communities, and planning theory. Meyerson, with wide experience in the city planning field, had been on the staffs of the American Society of Planning Officials, the Philadelphia City Planning Commission, and the Michael Reese Hospital.

This staff, together with the other members of the Committee on Planning from the various social science departments, developed a training program in planning that was unique in many ways and stemmed directly from the comprehensive approach to planning of those who had sponsored this new undertaking and of those who were to give it substance and reality.[4] By the fall of

4 Others also made contributions to the development of the Chicago Program as members of the planning staff. Among them were William Ludlow, who gave several courses on planning techniques during 1947-48 and 1948-49; Julius Margolis, who did research on planning standards and on social accounting and gave courses on urban land use and national income accounting

1948 a special curriculum had been prepared, there was a staff to teach the planning "core" courses and to lead the planning workshops, and the Committee on Planning was given the power to recommend degrees for both the Master of Arts and the Doctor of Philosophy in planning.

II *The Intellectual Basis for Planning*

The faculty members who taught within the Chicago Planning Program had diverse research interests and held quite different social and political views. All agreed, however, that the chief task for planning education lay in the development of basic planning principles. It was clear to the Chicago group that there was need for research which would lead to the development of general principles applicable not in one situation alone, but, with modifications, in any similar one. For endless time and effort are saved by not having to evolve new techniques for every new situation.

Actual research findings cannot, of course, be described here. All that can be done is to present a very brief and formal outline of the research undertaken by the planning staff.[5]

RESEARCH ON CITIES AND REGIONS

The effort to develop basic principles was made largely within the context of practical developmental problems. Much of the

---

during 1949 to 1952; and David Wallace and Isaac Green, who taught in the Planning Program for relatively brief periods but contributed to the development of the core courses in city planning. Richard L. Meier joined the planning staff in 1950. Meier had worked as an industrial chemist and had been executive secretary of the Federation of American Scientists. His knowledge of many scientific and technological fields contributed importantly to the Program, and particularly to the planning workshops. In addition, several city planners, among them Walter Blucher and Dennis O'Harrow of the American Society of Planning Officials, taught within the Program on a part-time basis.

5 See Appendix III-B, p. 168, for a selected list of publications of the staff touching on the various subjects briefly mentioned in this section.

research of the planning staff focused on those fields in which planning was already widely used as a basic approach to the solution of group problems: the city and the region. City planning was concerned primarily with shaping the habitat or physical environment of urban man. Regional planning was more immediately concerned with the ways in which natural resources could be brought into the service of man's needs and economic development processes facilitated. These elements were central also in considering the development problems of the economically less-advanced countries of the world.

Theory and practice came together in an effort to arrive at a deeper understanding of the problems of cities and regions and of ways of overcoming them. Intensive investigation centered on the structure and problems of American cities, including physical patterns,[6] social structure, and urban politics and administration. Special attention was devoted to problems of physical and social change as expressed in urban redevelopment and urban renewal, the problems of industrial siting, and the problems of housing. For regions and underdeveloped areas, major concern centered on the forces generating economic growth, on resource conservation and use, on the influence of population growth and population control, on the application of new technology to problems of world food and fuel needs and resources,[7] and on the planned provision of public services and facilities.[8]

PLANNING THEORY

The theoretical underpinning of planning was felt to be of the greatest immediate importance. It was necessary to define and delimit the *core* of this relatively new field of study.

From the first, the Chicago group used "planning" as a generic term to refer broadly to the ways in which men and women, act-

---

[6] Here the actual and potential contributions of design, architecture, and engineering were studied.

[7] Cf. Richard L. Meier, *Science and Economic Development: New Patterns of Living* (New York: Wiley & The Technology Press, 1956).

[8] A book on "The Long-Range Planning of Governmental Activities" is in preparation by Harvey S. Perloff and Richard L. Meier.

ing through organized entities, endeavor to guide developments so as to solve the pressing problems around them and approximate the vision of the future which they hold.

A plan sets guidelines for future action, and planning involves the careful elaboration and integration of a series of projected actions to attain the desired goals. Planning thus centers on the making of decisions and scheduled effectuation of policies.[9] It takes form in a number of closely integrated steps, from the analysis of problems, the setting of broad objectives and the survey of available resources, to the establishment of specific operating targets; and through various succeeding stages until the results can be checked against the targets established and needed adjustments proposed.

It was seen that an understanding of the nature, potentialities, and limitations of planning could be arrived at only by study in depth at the most critical points in the process and by examining the process within concrete social situations. In this way, practical or professional training—aside from its educational values— could be a means of securing deeper understanding of the planning process by drawing out of planning practice those general principles which would seem to apply in most planning situations. Conversely, the combination of the theoretical and practical could also be a way of adding to professional training the insights obtained by focusing attention on the theoretical elements.

Study of the planning process brought to the fore questions of how societies (groups, organizations, firms, communities, nations) make arrangements for the future, and of methods and techniques for translating broad social values and objectives into "operational" terms which relate means to ends in logical sequences. These considerations led staff members to a detailed study of old and new planning techniques, such as the "master plan," the "development plan," and long-range financial planning and, more generally, of alternative ways in which day-by-day decisions could be guided toward the longer-range goals of society

9 Cf. Martin Meyerson and Edward C. Banfield, *Politics, Planning and the Public Interest: The Case of Public Housing in Chicago* (Glencoe, Ill.: The Free Press, 1955); Rexford G. Tugwell, "The Utility of the Future in the Present," *Public Administration Review*, Vol. 8 (Winter 1948), pp. 49–59.

within the framework of problem situations about which various interests and groups are concerned.

Closely related to these issues is the problem of public choice. A key question is this: How can societies make the best possible choices in order to achieve a variety of group ends (sometimes conflicting in nature)? Here are encountered problems of optimization and allocation of resources among various public activities according to objective standards rather than solely on the basis of political pressure. The search for principles led into a detailed examination of the theory of public budgeting and study of standards, priorities, and requirements in planning.

All of these questions bring planning theory into close association with theory in political science, economics, sociology, anthropology, geography, statistics, and philosophy, and much of the research by the planning staff was carried out in collaboration with colleagues in the various social science disciplines.

Particular interest centered on the long-term commitments by communities. For example, how does one best allocate highly limited urban space to various functions and activities? Also, what may be preferred methods for allocating resources within the capital (or public investment) budget in providing for various community services? It was not expected that complete answers could be found for these questions, at least not as they exist in the real world; but through the exercise of logic and analysis combined with the known characteristics of various institutions and techniques, ways through which the planning process might be improved could become apparent.

OTHER RESEARCH

Other essentials of planning with which the planning staff was concerned were: (1) means of bringing to bear effectively the content and techniques of the different fields of natural, social, and technical sciences and of aesthetics in the analysis of planning tasks and in the preparation of plans; (2) social organization, and specifically the dynamics of group decision making and community participation and attitudes; and (3) technology as related to planning, including the social implications of new technology and the ways in which new technology might be applied to the solution of planning problems.

In most of these areas of planning research only small beginnings were made. At a minimum, however, the research of the staff served to enrich and enliven the planning courses and workshops and to open up potentially fruitful areas of both positive and normative study.

III *The Training Program*

THE PLANNING CURRICULUM

An attempt was made to fuse theory and practice in the training program as it developed over the years.[10] Every student, whether he would eventually concentrate his training in city planning or in regional planning, was obliged to take three courses—Planning Theory, Socio-economic Elements of Planning, and Physical Elements of Planning—which together made up the first phase of the *core curriculum.* (See figure 1.) These were taken at the beginning of his studies. With this general background fresh in his mind, he would be ready to undertake his more specialized work for which he could select either city planning or planning for regions and underdeveloped areas. Education in each of these fields was rounded out by a workshop in which a group of students working as a team attempted to solve an empirical planning problem. Finally, toward the close of their stay in the

10 The philosophy underlying planning education in the Chicago Program is discussed in Harvey S. Perloff, "How Shall We Train the Planners We Need?" *Planning 1951, Proceedings of the Annual Planning Conference, October 14–17, 1951* (Chicago: American Society of Planning Officials, 1952), pp. 13–22.

Opposite: FIGURE 1. *Examples of Courses of Instruction Leading to a Two-Year M.A. Degree in Planning*

PLANNING

	Planning Theory	Socio-Economic Elements of Planning	Physical Elements of Planning
Core courses	Planning Theory	Socio-Economic Elements of Planning	Physical Elements of Planning

City Planning	(or)	*Regional Planning*

Courses in field of concentration

City Planning	Regional Planning
Site Planning and Design	Economic & Resource Development
Principles of City Planning	Contemporary Resource Management
Urban Land-Use	Rural Land-Use Planning
City Planning Adm. & Law	Techniques of Resources Utilization
City Planning Workshop	Regional Planning Workshop

Core: co-ordinative workshop

Co-ordinative Workshop combining city and regional aspects in a practical planning problem.

Electives — To complete a total of 18 course credits (normally taken in a two-year period).

RELATED FIELD

A minimum of four courses in *one* of the following fields (to develop solid competence in at least one of the social or technical sciences):

Anthropology
Economics
Geography
Political Science
Sociology
Architecture *
Engineering *
Law

(These courses were to have a specific "focus." Thus, a student taking a minor in Political Science might focus his studies on Public Administration; a Geography minor might concentrate on transportation studies or on urban land-use.)

* In most cases involved credit given for previous studies in a technical school.

program, city and regional planners were once again brought together in an intensive "co-ordinative" workshop (the last phase of the core curriculum) in which a wide range of planning knowledge could be brought together and applied in a practical problem.

The workshops were one of the key features of planning education at Chicago. There the student would become accustomed to work as a member of a planning team. He would be taught how to apply his previous learning—as acquired from lectures, seminar discussions, and wide reading—in a realistic situation. And by no means least in importance, practical research in the workshops would suggest new hypotheses for exploration. The workshops provided an opportunity for testing abstract principles; they also fructified theoretical speculations in ways that were often revealing.

All of the workshops dealt with practical reality. Some were chosen because of the interest inherent in the problem and because

FIGURE 2   *Examples of Planning Workshops*

City planning	Regional planning	Co-ordinative workshop
A Preliminary Plan for the Andrew Corporation and the Orland Park Community	Cost-Benefit Analysis of the St. Lawrence Seaway Project	A General Plan for the Development of the Columbia Basin, Including Urban Expansion
A Preliminary Plan for the Development of the Hyde Park-Kenwood Community	Master Planning for Industry in Puerto Rico	Master Planning for Transportation in Puerto Rico: Intraurban and Interurban
Transportation in the University of Chicago Community	Development of Irrigation Facilities in the Columbia Basin	Industrial Location in the Chicago Metropolitan Region
Extension of a Satellite Community in the Chicago Metropolitan Area	Performance Budgeting for Developmental Planning in Israel	Forest Resources and Forest Utilization in the South: 1955–75, a study in projection

adequate materials were available. (For example, work on the Columbia Basin could draw on dozens of volumes of published materials.) Other workshops were conducted under contractual arrangement with a professional planning body or other organization interested in having preliminary or supporting studies made for decisions that had to be faced.[11] A partial list of workshops will perhaps indicate the range that was covered.

Planning courses formed only part of the total education of a planner at the University of Chicago. For a Master's degree, no less than four courses were required in some one field other than planning, such as geography, sociology, political science, or economics (in addition to a choice of at least two or three "electives"). A detailed acquaintance with the theory and research techniques of at least one other academic field was thought to be an indispensable requirement in the education of a planner. Planning theory and practice were drawing on a number of academic disciplines and professional fields of work. The young planner could not, in the short period of his university career, be expected to gain mastery of all the relevant fields. He might however learn about one. This would give him a direct insight into the knowledge and technique a person specializing in one of the academic disciplines could be expected to have; he would need this type of insight in working as a planner with specialists from a variety of fields. Such training would also give him a base for his own specialized training—either at school or on the job.

Beyond the Master's degree, students were accepted for a doctorate in planning. A student who had obtained a Ph.D. in planning would be primarily a research worker, a teacher of other planners, or a person prepared for responsible positions in government. The requirements included these: (1) knowledge and competence in the field of planning equivalent to the Master of Arts level to start with; (2) active participation in an advanced planning seminar running for two quarters; (3) preparation of a research paper and its presentation to the seminar; (4) a planning

11 There were, however, certain dangers involved in contract work. The limitations set by the necessity of turning out an "acceptable" report could cripple originality and inhibit exploratory reaching out into new fields. This always had to be balanced against the gains of working in a "real" situation.

"specialization" acquired by advanced work in a field such as housing, social survey, resource analysis and management, budgetary and financial planning, planning design, or transportation; and (5) submission of a dissertation, constituting an original contribution to planning, in proof of his capacity as a researcher.

THE STUDENTS IN THE PLANNING PROGRAM

Ninety-nine students registered for a degree in planning at the University of Chicago between 1948 (when planning degrees began to be offered) and 1955–56.[12] Slightly more than half concentrated on regional planning, while the remainder sought a degree in city planning. Almost one-fifth of the students were from foreign countries.[13] In addition to these planning "majors," some forty students took a large share of their training in the Planning Program while working toward their degrees in other departments and committees.

By the time the Program came to a close, at the end of the 1955–56 school year, 58 Master of Arts degrees in Planning had been awarded (28 in city planning; 30 in regional planning); 6 Ph.D. degrees (5 in regional planning); and an additional 24 students had passed all academic requirements for a doctorate but had not yet completed their theses (7 concentrating on city planning and 17 on regional planning). Most of the doctoral candidates took regional planning as their "field of concentration." Jobs in the regional field were available to Ph.D.'s on a preferred basis. The same was not true of city planning; a Ph.D. in city planning was as yet quite rare and was not required to obtain a good job in the field.

As might be expected, a high proportion of the thesis topics chosen by the Ph.D. students dealt with problems of planning

12 Of the 99 students registered, 25 came with a Master's degree: 2 from architecture, 3 from engineering, 8 from economics, 5 from political science, 4 from sociology, 1 from geography, and 2 from social science.

13 From Canada (3), Puerto Rico (3), British territories (3), India (2), New Zealand, Jordan, Iran, Ethiopia, Yugoslavia, France, and China. In 1954–55, the proportion of foreign students to the total number of planning students reached 40 per cent.

theory or with regional economic development. The actual titles may be of interest:

Titles of completed and accepted Ph.D. theses:

1. "The Spatial Structure of Economic Development in the Tennessee Valley" (J. Friedmann)
2. "Planning for a Metropolitan University" (L. Thompson)
3. "Obtaining Information from Outside the Society for Planned Economic Development, with Special Reference to India" (A. Gheselayagh)
4. "New Technology and the Supply of Petroleum; the Treatment of Uncertainty in Resource Planning" (M. Spangler)
5. "Government and the Depressed Area; A Study of Government Operations in Relation to the Economy and Population of Southern Illinois" (M. Levin)
6. "Factors of Economic Development of an Underdeveloped Area; Illustrated by World Relationships to the Okovango Delta in Africa" (D. Randall)

Ph.D. thesis topics approved, but not yet completed:

1. "Role of Agro-aeronautics in Rural Land-Use Planning (D. Carr)
2. "Decision-making Setting in Educational Planning" (J. Dyckman)
3. "Analysis and Projection in the Economy of the Metropolitan Region" (B. Harris)
4. "Planning for Urban Renewal in Puerto Rico" (J. Heikoff)
5. "Planned Opportunities for Personal Achievement in Old Age within the Local Community: An Exploratory Case Study in a Chicago Housing Authority Project" (W. Nixon)
6. "Planning Urban Development in British Columbia" (I. Robinson)
7. "Economic Growth and Organization of Scientific Research: The Water Resources of the Indian Sub-Continent" (C. Seipp)
8. "The Development of Standards for Planning" (R. Sterba)
9. "Workers' Management in the Industrial Enterprise in Yugo-

slavia: A Study of the Firm in Yugoslav Economic Planning" (R. Trees)

10. "Population Growth and Economic Development Planning" (J. Urner)

Whatever the shortcomings of the Chicago Planning Program may have been—and there were many—from the very beginning it was able to attract not only a sizable number of students, but also an unusual proportion of outstanding students. The experimental atmosphere of the Chicago planning school was clearly an attraction for a certain type of mature graduate student.

It is interesting to note that during most of the years that the Chicago Program was in existence, it had the largest number of students of any planning school in the United States.

A significant indication of the caliber of students attracted into the Planning Program was provided by statistics furnished by the Dean of Students in 1954. These data were concerned with entrants into the Social Science Division from the College of the University of Chicago during recent previous years. They showed the proportion of those with average grades of B and better during their college careers, and those below this level. The highest proportion of B-and-better students of the total entering any unit of the Division was in the Planning Program (75 per cent); the Department of Economics was second with 56 per cent; and the other departments in the Division ranged below, down to 13 per cent. No other equally clear-cut indications of the caliber of students attracted to the Planning Program can be given, but the grade records made by the planning students in other departments is impressive.

Some of the students had, of course, quite ordinary abilities and aspirations; they wanted the training that would enable them to get and hold a job in a planning agency. But a surprising number were in a group which Richard Meier has aptly characterized as "persons who want to do good competently." These were students who often carried a full school load while holding down a difficult outside job. They did not avoid the more demanding courses such as advanced statistics, demography, mathematical economics, and social research, but often made such courses the main part of their minor field. And they met informally but seriously, frequently after long hours in workshops, to discuss the more difficult problems in planning, and thereby learned how to learn from each other.

With only one or two exceptions, the students trained in the Program have stayed in the planning field. The jobs they have taken cover a wide range. Almost all of the students who were trained in city planning have gone into urban planning agencies of one type or another. They are found, or have been, in city or county planning units in Milwaukee, Philadelphia, Louisville, Washington, D.C., St. Petersburg, El Paso, Guilford, Westchester County, Providence, Cincinnati, Chicago, and elsewhere. They are found in housing agencies, redevelopment agencies, and in new urban renewal agencies. Two students are with the Federal Housing and Home Finance Administration. Several are with private planning consulting firms, or have started consulting firms of their own. It is, of course, difficult to determine the quality of the work done by the Chicago graduates. But unusual contributions here and there can be spotted. Contacts with graduates have indicated that quite a number of them are reaching out for significant improvements in approach and methodology; many have learned to use research as a powerful planning tool; some have shown qualities of inventiveness and originality.

The Chicago Program graduates who specialized in regional planning have also gone into a variety of jobs. Several are, or were, with state and regional planning and development agencies, such as the Rhode Island State Development Board, the Tennessee State Planning Commission, the Tennessee Valley Authority, the Puerto Rico Planning Board. Some are, or were, with federal agencies: the Technical Review Staff of the Department of the Interior, the Federal Reserve Board, the Bureau of Standards, the Bureau of Reclamation. With only one known exception, the foreign students have returned to their home countries to take up posts for which they have been trained.

Possibly the most striking feature is the number that have gone into research positions. Several are doing research at universities. For example, a high proportion of the research posts within the Institute of Urban Studies at the University of Pennsylvania are filled by Chicago planning graduates. A few of the graduates are with nonprofit research organizations, such as the Midwest Research Institute at Kansas City, Mo., and the Stanford Research Institute. One graduate is now professor of regional planning in Brazil on an appointment with the International Co-operation Administration. Three other former students are teaching planning, one at the University of British Columbia, two at the University of Pennsylvania.

The large number of graduates who are devoting themselves directly to the task of developing and advancing the planning field is a significant measure of the effectiveness of the Chicago Program. But crucial immediate planning tasks also have to be carried out competently; the large number of front-line planning positions being held by Chicago graduates is another type of "payoff" of no small importance.

IV *Evaluative Comments*

Someone who has been involved in an educational experiment is not himself in a position to provide a balanced and objective evaluation of the experiment. However, evaluative comments highlighting key aspects of such an educational effort can provide an "inside" view which may be of interest to others concerned with the same field of endeavor. Within this framework, several facets of the Chicago experiment seem particularly pertinent.

THE INTERDEPARTMENTAL QUESTION

From the beginning, a serious set of problems centered on the question of the relation of the Planning Program to the departments of the Social Science Division. The various faculty members who in 1945 had urged the establishment of a planning curriculum within the Division had assumed that it would be an interdepartmental effort in which faculty from the various disciplines would join in providing courses and seminars and in undertaking research in planning. They expected that the only new person to be brought in specifically to this effort would himself be appointed to one of the existing departments. Mr. Tugwell, however, regarded planning as a rather separate field of study which, to flourish, should draw together a number of new full-time persons, with training in the contributing disciplines but chiefly interested in planning, into a relatively independent planning group.[14]

When the Divisional Committee on Planning—made up of representatives from the various departments—began to think concretely of the implications of their notions for a planning curriculum, they finally recognized that a number of full-time individuals must be attached to the program to give the core courses and to supervise the workshops, which constituted a time-consuming responsibility. Nevertheless a feeling lingered that the departmental faculty should play a more important role in the planning program—despite the limited time that individual members could devote to an interdepartmental effort. This, of course, is fairly typical of problems that dog all interdisciplinary activities, but if general financial stringency had not set in, it is likely that the halfway arrangement which was actually evolved (i.e., a small core staff and much reliance on courses and seminars given by the various departments [15]) would have turned out to

[14] Later, when I became director of the Planning Program (in 1951), the planning staff made an especially concentrated effort to work out closer arrangements with the various social science departments, and found this to be a difficult, but profitable, endeavor. (H.S.P.)

[15] Many planning courses were developed in conjunction with other departments. Examples of such "joint" courses were: National Income and Related Aggregates (Economics); Community Planning Administration and Law (Political Science); Urban Land Use (Geography); Rural Land Use Planning (Geography); Theory of Democratic Planning (Political Science); Planning by Community Agencies (Sociology); Contemporary Problems in Underdeveloped Areas (History) The Chicago Region (Geography); Modern Real Estate (Law); Freedom Under Planning (Political Science); Clinic in the Problems of Metropolitan Chicago (Political Science and Geography); Building Codes (Law); Contemporary Resource Management Problems (Geography).

be a truly effective arrangement for the handling of a planning curriculum grounded mainly in the social sciences.

UNIQUE CIRCUMSTANCES

Certain special circumstances, in addition to those to do with money, affected the entire operation. One was the fact that the planning experiment was undertaken in a university which has neither a school of architecture nor a school of engineering. Individuals with a design background who were brought into the Program to teach the physical aspects of planning found the Social Science Division a stimulating but quite "foreign" environment, and inevitably they felt isolated and apart from others intimately concerned with their specialty. Such persons did not stay on at the University very long and, as a consequence, the Planning Program never achieved a good balance between the social science and physical aspects of planning.

As a matter of fact, the entire environment within which the Planning Program functioned was quite "special." The Social Science Division of the University of Chicago was as extreme an environment for planning education in one direction as is the usual school of architecture or engineering in the other. There is what might be called an "ecological" (or normal adjustment) factor here. Just as original theoretical work does not usually flourish in most purely technical schools, so in the case of the Social Science Division, applied professional work, while possible, was not exactly honored. The Planning Program had embarked on an approach which left it in an uncomfortably exposed middle position. It could not, nor did it, lay claim to being a separate social science discipline with all the prerogatives of a "new science." Nor was it clearly a professional program in a professional school, in a comparable position with a school of business or law or architecture. The Chicago planning group wanted the best of both worlds without entirely sacrificing either. As a result, it did not fully satisfy anyone.

Most planning schools in the United States had placed themselves on the side of "job orientation," emphasizing the applied aspects of planning. It is for this reason that nearly all planning curricula are located in schools of architecture, design, or engineering, where the whole institutional matrix is pervaded by an atmosphere of action and practical creativeness.

This, of course, has its drawbacks, and to overcome them it was decided at Chicago to foster an intimate relationship between planning and the social sciences. Design was only one of several aspects of planning; the others had to be given equal attention. Also, it seemed questionable whether a few isolated courses in economics, sociology, geography, and so forth, when merely ancillary to design and job-oriented training, would suffice for an adequate grounding on the part of the students in the sciences of society. The student had to obtain a really deep understanding of the relations of planned action to the social phenomena on which the scholars in social science were throwing an ever sharper and clearer light.

But the task of creating the basis for what was essentially a new approach to planning education, with an emphasis on broadly applicable theory and principles, was extremely difficult and progress was far from spectacular. It was not easy to explain to those in another planning tradition just what was involved in the newer experimental approach, and many members of the planning profession were certain that the Chicago Program was training planners for anything but a practical world. Actually, it was true that in the pressure to develop a theoretical base for planning, the applied and professional aspects of planning were not given as much, or as "devoted," attention as they deserved. The "atmosphere" of the Social Science Division made this almost inevitable.

On the other side of the picture, a certain number of the social science faculty were uneasy about planning education within the Division. They felt that the Division should devote its resources to advancing theory in the basic social science disciplines. Professional training and study of the applied aspects of the social sciences seemed to them a diversion. While this may not have represented a majority opinion and while many members of the Division favored the planning effort, nevertheless the planning staff often had the feeling of being on the defensive.

What is especially evident from this experience—as well as from the experience of a number of other professional fields—

is that it is extremely difficult to combine theoretical work and professional training, particularly in an early stage of a field's development. Those concerned with the practical problems of city and regional planning, and with preparing students for dealing with these problems, normally find it difficult to do the type of research that can advance theory. On the other side, those who get deeply involved in theoretical considerations tend to become more and more remote from the concerns of practical planners. This is far from a unique problem, but it is a particularly difficult one for planning at this stage in its development. A minimum condition for coping with the problem is certainly a full awareness of its existence and nature.

SOME ISSUES FOR PLANNING AND
FOR THE SOCIAL SCIENCES

The Chicago experiment in planning education undoubtedly raised more questions than it answered, and its major value may lie precisely in bringing out some basic issues for the planning profession, for social scientists, and for educators in general.

The Chicago Program, more than any other, confronted the planning profession with the question of whether it was satisfied with a training essentially apprenticeship in nature—a passing on of the planning arts. It sharply raised the issue of whether any field has a right to separate existence in the academic world unless it can develop a unique core curriculum representing the basic principles and approach of the field. It raised more forcibly than before the question of the appropriate role of the social sciences in planning education. It also raised the issue of the relationship between training in city planning and in other fields of planning, an issue which the Chicago experiment itself did very little to resolve.[16]

16 As suggested in Parts I and II, the requirements for training regional planners differ significantly from those involved in training city planners. It is obvious that much additional experimentation with planning education will be needed before it can be known if, and under what circumstances, training for the various fields of planning can be combined.

The Chicago Planning Program also highlighted some significant issues for social science. None of them is especially new, but the problem of planning education brings them rather sharply forward. Can new insights into social structure and social behavior be developed by directly examining ways in which collective decisions can be made more rational? Are concentrated efforts to develop projective techniques a legitimate enterprise for the social sciences, that is, can social science be applied to the future as well as to the past? Does it make sense to devote scholarly attention to the elaboration of "operational" links between social and behavioral analysis on the one side and social policy formation on the other?

V Problems for Planning Research

Cannot the existing social science disciplines themselves deal adequately with the intellectual problems mentioned in the previous section? Must a new field of study be developed (whether under the name of planning or some other title) in order to cope with them? The answer would seem to be that the basic social science disciplines can, of course, deal with problems of this type; some individual scholars in the various disciplines have, in fact, long been concerned with such matters. However, the "dynamics" of organized intellectual endeavor must also be recognized. When young scholars find that both status and academic progress within their own discipline can best be achieved by concentrating on theoretical problems within that discipline, one cannot blame them for not venturing into interdisciplinary endeavors that often are risky.

This is a nice question for the educator, or student of education, as well as for the social scientist. How do we see to it that important intellectual problems are tackled even when they are so difficult that research progress must inevitably be slow and individual scholars can enter the intellectual fray only at the expense of their own career progress?

It may well be that the planning schools (or at least the better ones among them), because of their particular orientation, have an opportunity at the present time to make important academic contributions, by developing new approaches to the analysis and solution of some types of social problems. At the same time, as the other side of the coin, unless the existing planning schools reach out for such academic leadership, they may be unable to compete with other fields for the better students.

It is likely, as a practical matter, that the present planning schools can go varying distances in the direction of undertaking this type of advanced research endeavor. There may yet remain need for the establishment of one or more new experimental centers directly geared to probing into these relatively neglected subjects.[17] This is too large a subject to be treated adequately here. But perhaps it will be suggestive to set down some of the topics and problems—covering both positive and normative elements—in the study of which planning schools with powerful research arms might well make significant contributions, working closely with scholars from other fields of study.

POTENTIALLY FRUITFUL SUBJECTS FOR RESEARCH

1. *The nature of the planning process.* The study of planning as an ongoing organizational or group function, of planning behavior, of the potentialities and limitations of the planning process and of rational action—this is at the heart of planning theory. This topic has been discussed earlier (pages 141–43) and it remains only to underline the fact that no more than a small beginning has been made in providing an understanding of "ra-

17 It is interesting to note Norbert Wiener's comment in his introduction to *Cybernetics: Or Control and Communication in the Animal and the Machine* (New York: John Wiley and Sons, 1949). ". . . The most fruitful areas for the growth of the sciences were those which had been neglected as a no-man's land between the various established fields. . . ."

tional" group action, and very much obviously remains to be done.

2. *"Social design."* This is a companion subject to creative physical design which has long been a concern of the planning schools (as well as of architects, landscape architects, and engineers). Important new insights might be gained by careful study of the problems of evolving new institutions and of new approaches aimed at the solution of social problems, particularly problems which are essentially environmental or developmental in nature. This is not a question of searching for actual solutions to actual problems, but the "theory" of how a group might go about designing social means which would have a high probability of solving a given class of problems. Topics to be studied might include questions of evaluative techniques (or how society might maximize what it can learn from past efforts), questions of the circumstances under which social experimentation is feasible and necessary, and questions of how creative solutions to social problems might be made the concern of the largest possible number of groups rather than solely of a government.

There may be some possibilities in the extension of "operations research" approaches and the development of what might be called "social operations research." The relation of this kind of study to planning is obvious, but the planning schools have not yet seriously approached the search for creative solutions except in relation to creative design solutions. Some would argue that all of the social sciences are involved in such a study but, as a matter of actual fact, the social science disciplines at the present time normally tend to stop short of the task of evolving practical alternative solutions to the problems with which they deal.

An important aspect of "social design" is the study of what might be called "organizational competence." Quite often an activity or function is shifted from the private sphere to public operations, or from local government to central government, mainly because the alternatives have been posed in extreme form and little thought has been given to organizational competence for achieving social objectives. A case in point arises where the central government in an underdeveloped country will undertake the entrepreneurial function in the economy because private enterprise is not flourishing, without seriously investigating means of nurturing private entrepreneurship so as to maximize over time the sources of new ideas and new investment. Another case in point is the shift of mass transit in a city from private ownership to public, without testing whether this is the most efficient way of providing the subsidy to mass transportation which seems to be required.

It is a matter of coming to understand "Who Can Do What Best?" In any given culture, each of the major types of institutions normally can achieve some kind of social objectives better than can the other institutions, but can attain other objectives only under very costly arrangements, if at all. Thus, to take an obvious example, a locality may not be able to foster full employment, but it can give many persons experience in the management of public affairs. A better understanding of organizational competence can provide the basis for organizational arrangements—including joint arrangements—which can simultaneously approximate a number of social objectives rather than force society to choose among valued objectives because choices tend to be presented in the form of extremes.

3. *The effective combination of procedure and content in both education and governmental practice.* Here planning has a special advantage since in many instances in actual operations this combination characterizes planning. Thus, in many cities today the planning agency is a staff arm of the chief executive and is concerned with many procedural matters as well as with the actual analysis of urban problems and the recommendation of specific solutions. To date, the academic study of public administration has largely focused on procedure or process; other social science fields and the applied sciences have chiefly emphasized content. Planning studies and planning education might well develop ways of bringing these together in the solution of clusters of problems, such as those involved in the physical development of the city or those involved in the optimum development of a resources region. Master planning and programming are examples of subjects that almost inevitably involve a combination of procedure and content, and the study of such subjects —preferably in co-operation with students of public administration—holds high promise of advancing the effectiveness of public

operations. In fact, there is much to be said in favor of developing a certain number of what might be called "programs of public affairs" which would be concerned with problems of both content (policy) and procedures and which would join the study of public administration and the study of planning.

4. *The relation of technology to the creation and solution of social problems.* Here again is an important field which in the main has fallen in between the various academic fields and which is of direct concern to planning. Technology, at one and the same time, has been a major source of social change and of social problems; it is also in actuality, and even more potentially, one of the most important means for the solution of social problems. On both counts it has caused contemporary planners the most embarrassment in their assessment of what may be desirable futures. Given the nature of our present world, there is need for intensive study of social techniques for the development and application of new scientific and engineering ideas to the solution of major social problems. Investigation is also required regarding possible methods for predicting, directing, and controlling the effects of technological change. Science tends to "telegraph its punches," and it may well be possible to get the optimum returns from science by learning more about the fruitful application of technology to the solution of difficult social problems and by learning more about predicting and preventing dislocation from technological developments.

5. *Projective techniques.* All plans—whether by individuals, private groups, or government—and all policy formulation must be based on some assumptions about the future. The effectiveness of such planning and policy formulation is therefore dependent, in part at least, on the soundness of the projections employed. The future is not knowable in the same sense that the past is, but there are certain kinds of knowledge that can optimize the opportunities for achieving the goals set. Thus, for example, more can be known about the degree of risk involved in various classes of endeavors, in the same way that insurance rates are set to provide for an uncertain future. There are many statistical and nonstatistical problems in projection that deserve detailed attention. While almost all sciences are concerned with this question, and important gains are being recorded in individual fields,

only a small beginning has been made in developing projection as a basic tool of planning and policy formulation.

RESEARCH IN THE PHYSICAL AND DESIGN ELEMENTS

All of the topics discussed here fall within the general scope of the social sciences. This is clearly only part of the story. Equally challenging problems with a direct bearing on planning fall within the scope of the natural and technical sciences. Many potentially fruitful subjects for research with a planning focus must draw upon the knowledge and techniques of engineering, architecture, landscape architecture, geography, geology, mathematics, and the various natural sciences. One can think of the rich possibilities that can be developed through research relating planning to construction and transportation defined in their most basic elements as "shelter" and "movement." But this is a large subject by itself and outside my own competence. Its importance must, however, be recorded here.

POTENTIAL ROLE OF PLANNING STUDY

Society and human behavior are much too complex to be studied in their totality by any one science or discipline or approach. The family of sciences—"pure," "basic," "applied," "technical," and in between—is necessarily made up of individual specializations, each trying to understand a different aspect of human existence and its nonhuman environment. However, as a consequence of the drive to understand more deeply these complicated individual aspects of life and environment, many rather critical questions fall outside the purview of all the established fields. These tend to be precisely the questions involving *many* aspects of social life and physical environment and questions dealing with "wholes" more than with parts, as is the case with so many problems and issues in social policy. Educators (as well as citizens) are much concerned with this problem. Efforts at solution take the form of all types of new interdisciplinary programs of study, extensions of general education, the bringing together of scholars in joint research projects, and the like. Each has its own particular advantages and disadvantages; none can hope to be an ultimate answer.

It is in this framework that the potentialities of planning studies and planning education can best be seen. Planning offers certain kinds of advantages that can be built upon. The fact is that planning practice urgently needs answers to questions concerning ways of making social decisions more rational and of projecting and studying the future. Thus, once a planning school reaches out for general principles and theory, its faculty can be expected to become directly involved with precisely these questions. Planning study involves a mixed theoretical-applied, art-science approach, more or less in the same sense as the study of medicine, law, architecture, and other professional fields. The application of research findings, as well as of creative social and physical design elements, to problem solving and program formulation is clearly an art-science. Possibly the most unique feature of planning study is the conscious consideration of the desirable and possible as well as the existing and probable. The practical problems with which professional planners have to struggle serve to define the questions for planning research so that in an appropriate academic environment such research would tend to bring useful new perspectives to the study of social man and his environment.

An important problem, however, does remain: Can a school or program that is mainly geared to professional training attract to itself absolutely first-rate theoretical minds? Will such persons be willing to give "practical" courses? Will they be frightened away by the fact that most students will be much more interested in "practical" rather than in theoretical problems? Clearly there is no ready answer.

Much undoubtedly depends on the ability of planning schools to develop very close ties with the basic social science disciplines, as well as with technical schools. The planning schools might well provide a home for scholars from various disciplines who become intrigued by certain social problems with interdisciplinary and theoretical-applied elements. Such scholars might be brought in as full-time or part-time teachers, as full-time or temporary research personnel, as members of a joint (team) research project, as members of a joint seminar, or as participants in planning symposia or in a lecture series. There is much to be gained by functioning through such a loose and changing federation of scholars, rather than by the creation of academic empires. Planning study gains most by continually refreshing itself rather than by building in upon itself. The *core* concept is directly applicable here. It is a mistake to interpret professionalization (in general, but particularly in planning) as meaning the development of a narrow, well-defined boundary around a field. Rather, it should involve the development of a solid core of basic principles and methods at the center, and a reaching out at the edges for all sorts of ties with other fields of study. Thus, a planning school must have a core staff, just as it must have a series of core courses. However, the various members of the core faculty should have close ties with related departments and schools, and members of other departments should be able to come in and out in what has been called a "loose federation."

Planning study would seem to offer special advantages for the development of useful new approaches to the analysis and solution of social problems. This is a matter worthy of continued academic experimentation.

Appendix III–A *Degree Requirements:*
Program of Education and Research in
Planning, University of Chicago, 1954–55

Master of Arts

A candidate for the Master of Arts degree in Planning is required to develop a course of studies made up of three elements:

1. *The Planning core-curriculum,* consisting of three courses and one (two-course credit) workshop. The core courses are: Introduction to the Theory of Planning, Socio-economic Elements of Planning, and Physical Elements of Planning.

The Planning Workshop involves the application of the subject matter of these and related courses and of planning techniques to the solution of practical planning problems.

2. *A related (minor) field,* involving a minimum of four courses in one of the social sciences (anthropology, economics, geography, political science, or sociology) or in an applied science (engineering or architecture).

3. *A field of concentration* (either city planning or regional and underdeveloped-areas planning) involving a minimum of four courses and one specialized (two-course credit) workshop beyond the courses listed above.

I. THE CITY PLANNING FIELD OF CONCENTRATION

(a) The final examination on the field of concentration will be based mainly on the content of the following courses: 201, Site Planning and Design Laboratory; 304, Principles of City Planning; 314, Urban Land Use; 315, Physical Structure of the City; and 352–353, Workshop Problems of City Planning. Students who have or can acquire knowledge of the subject matter independently may not need to take the courses.

(b) The following additional courses are particularly relevant for the city planning concentration:

In the Planning Program: Planning of Governmental Services and Facilities; Housing; Methodology for Planning Research; City Government and Organization for Planning; City Planning Administration and Law.

In the Department of Geography: Urban Geography; Land Transportation; Ocean and Inland Water Transportation; Air Transportation; Industrial Localization; Clinic in Problems of Metropolitan Chicago; The Chicago Region; Map Drafting; Map, Photo, and Field Techniques.

In the Department of Sociology: Human Ecology; The Urban Community; Planning by Community Agencies; Field Studies; The Slum Community.

In the Department of Anthropology: The Family; Field Research in a Modern Community.

In the Department of Economics: Public Finance in the American Economy.

In the Department of Political Science: Public Administration—Organization and Management, Personnel, Responsibility; Administrative Regulation.

In the Department of Education: Social Trends and Educational Planning.

In the Division of the Social Sciences: Contemporary Urban and Rural Communities; Law and Community Development.

In the Law School: Modern Real Estate; Seminar—Building Codes; State and Local Governments.

II. THE REGIONAL AND UNDERDEVELOPED-AREAS FIELD OF CONCENTRATION

(a) The final examination on the field of concentration will be based mainly on the following courses: 303, Economic and Resource Development; 346, Rural Land-Use Planning; 348, Techniques of Resources Utilization; and 350–351, Workshop: Problems of Regional and Underdeveloped Areas Planning. Students who have or can acquire knowledge of the subject-matter independently may not need to take the courses.

(b) The following additional courses are particularly relevant for the regional and underdeveloped-areas concentration:

In the Planning Program: New Technology and Planning; Methodology for Planning Research; National Income and Related Aggregates.

In the Department of Geography: Physical Geography; Economic Geography; Conservation of Natural Resources; Geography of the Land; Map Drafting; Map, Photo, and Field Techniques; Contemporary Resource Management Problems.

In the Department of Economics: International Economics; Monetary Aspects of International Trade; Economic Aspects of International Relations; Monetary and Fiscal Policy; Choice and Possibilities in Economic Organization.

In the Department of Anthropology: Comparison of Cultures; Culture, Society, and the Individual; Cultural Dynamics (Action Anthropology).

In the Department of Political Science: The Politics of Agriculture; The Politics of Conservation.

In the Department of History: Development of Underdeveloped Areas.

In the Division of the Social Sciences: Seminar in Economic Development and Cultural Change.

Doctor of Philosophy

A candidate for the Doctor of Philosophy degree in Planning must normally possess, or acquire, knowledge and training equivalent to that required for the Master of Arts degree in Planning, and is required to develop an advanced course of studies consisting of the following elements:

1. *Advanced planning seminar.* Research papers and discussions of the central problems of planning.

2. *Planning specialization.* A minimum of three courses in a field of the student's choice providing advanced knowledge, techniques, and skills needed in developing professional competence and in making research contributions. Training in the specialization may be taken in one of the departments of the Division of the Social Sciences or in one of the neighboring educational institutions; or it may cut across existing disciplines. Illustrations of such fields of specialization are: Social Survey for Planning; Planning Administration; Resource Analysis and Management; Budgetary and Financial Planning; Production Management; Housing; Planning Law; Planning Design; Transportation Planning.

3. *Advanced courses* with special reference to foci of research, offered within and outside the Planning Program.

Planning Minor

Planning as a field of study (i.e. as a "minor" field) for students in other departments of the Division of the Social Sciences will consist of the three introductory courses in the core-curriculum, plus such additional courses in planning as would contribute to their research focus.

Appendix III–B   *Publications on Planning*

Subjects by Members of the Planning Staff,

University of Chicago, 1947–57

Represented are the writings of persons who had the most to do with the development of the University of Chicago ·Planning Program. In some cases the materials were published after the individual had left the University of Chicago, but in the main the materials were developed within the Planning Program.

Edward C. Banfield

BOOKS AND PAMPHLETS:
Government Project. Glencoe, Ill.: The Free Press, 1951.
(With Martin Meyerson.) *Politics, Planning and the Public Interest: The Case of Public Housing in Chicago.* Glencoe: The Free Press, 1955.
(With Morton Grodzins.) *Housing Policy and the Government of Metropolitan Areas.* New York: McGraw-Hill, forthcoming.

ARTICLES:
"Planning Under the Research and Marketing Act of 1946," *Journal of Farm Economics,* Vol. 31 (February 1949), 48–75.
"Congress and the Budget: A Planner's Criticism," *American Political Science Review,* Vol. 43 (December 1949), 1217–28.
(With R. G. Tugwell.) "Government Planning at Mid-Century," *Journal of Politics,* Vol. 13 (1951), 133–63.
(————.) "Grass Roots Democracy: Myth or Reality," *Public Administration Review,* Vol. 10 (Winter 1950), 47–55.
(————.) "The Planning Function Reappraised," *Journal of the American Institute of Planners,* Vol. 17 (Winter 1951), pp. 46–48.
"The Organization for Policy Planning in the U.S. Department of Agriculture," *Journal of Farm Economics,* Vol. 34 (February 1952), 14–34.

"The Politics of Metropolitan Area Organization," *Midwest Political Science Review* (forthcoming 1957).

Melville C. Branch, Jr.

BOOKS AND PAMPHLETS:

Aerial Photography in Urban Planning and Research. (Harvard City Planning Studies, Vol. 14.) Cambridge: Harvard University Press, 1948.

Local Planning Research. (Chairman, Research Committee, Southern Section, California Chapter, American Institute of Planners and the Bureau of Governmental Research.) Los Angeles: University of California at Los Angeles, 1956.

ARTICLES:

"Focus for Urban Planning," *Journal of Land and Public Utility Economics,* Vol. 23 (May 1947), 228–30.

"Coordinative Planning and the Architect," *Land Economics,* Vol. 26 (February 1950), 78–81.

"Concerning Coordinative Planning," *Journal of the American Institute of Planners,* Vol. 16 (Fall 1950), 163–71.

"Physical Aspects of City Planning," *Annals of the Association of American Geographers,* Vol. 41 (December 1951), 269–84.

"Psychological Factors in Business Planning," *Journal of the American Institute of Planners,* Vol. 22 (Summer 1956), 173–78.

"Conceptualization in Business Planning and Decision Making," *Journal of the American Institute of Planners,* Vol. 23 (Winter 1957), 13–21.

"Planning Environment for Research and Development," *The Princeton Engineer:* Part I (Environmental Considerations), Vol. 18 (October 1957); Part II (The Project Planning Process), Vol. 18 (November 1957).

Julius Margolis

ARTICLES:

"Public Works and Economic Stability," *Journal of Political Economy,* Vol. 57 (August 1949), 293–303.

"National Economic Accounting: Reorientation Needed," *Review of Economics and Statistics,* Vol. 34 (November 1952), 291–304.

"Benefits-Costs Analysis—Efficiency, Financial and Economic Feasibility, and External Economies," *Water Resources and Economic Development of the West*, Commission on Economics of Water Resources Development of the Western Agricultural Economics Research Council (July 1955).

"A Comment on the Pure Theory of Public Expenditures," *Review of Economics and Statistics*, Vol. 37 (November 1955), 347–56.

"Our Municipal Land Policy for Fiscal Gains," *National Tax Journal*, Vol. 9 (September 1956), 247–57.

"The Variation of Property Tax Rates within a Metropolitan Region," *National Tax Journal*, Vol. 9 (December 1956), 326–30.

"Fiscal Structure and Economic Activities within a Metropolitan Region," *Journal of Political Economy*, Vol. 65 (June 1957).

"Welfare Criteria and Efficient Pricing of Public Production," *Quarterly Journal of Economics*, Vol. 71 (August 1957).

Richard L. Meier

BOOKS AND PAMPHLETS:

Science and Economic Development: New Patterns of Living. New York: Wiley & The Technology Press of M.I.T., 1956.

Modern Science and the Human Fertility Problem, forthcoming.

(With Harvey S. Perloff.) Long Range Planning of Governmental Activities (in preparation).

ARTICLES:

"Industrialization of Photosynthesis and Its Social Effects," *Chemical and Engineering News*, Vol. 27 (1949), 3112–6.

"The Long-Term Prospects for Essential Minerals," *Bulletin of the Atomic Scientists*, Vol. 7 (August 1951), 214–16.

"Research as a Social Process: Social Status, Specialism and Technological Advance in Great Britain," *British Journal of Sociology*, Vol. 2 (June 1951) pp. 91–104; reprinted in *Research*, Vol. 4 (1951), 463–70.

(With A. K. Cairncross.) "New Industries and Economic Development in Scotland," *Three Banks Review*, No. 14 (June 1952), 3–21.

"Industrial Planning for Scotland: The Role of New Technology in the Economic Development of a Region," *Planning Outlook*, Vol. 2 (1952), 5–26.

"Automatic and Economic Development," *Bulletin of the Atomic Scientists*, Vol. 10 (April 1954), 129–33.

"The Economic and Social Consequences of the Growth in Application of Automatic Controls," *Institute of Radio Engineers Convention Record,* Part 4 (1955), 62–3.

"Automation in the American Economy," *Journal of Business,* Vol. 29 (January 1956), 14–27.

Martin Meyerson

BOOKS AND PAMPHLETS:

(With others.) *Urban Renewal Research Program.* New York: American Council to Improve our Neighborhoods, 3 volumes, 1954.

(With Edward C. Banfield.) *Politics, Planning and the Public Interest: The Case of Public Housing in Chicago.* Glencoe: The Free Press, 1955.

ARTICLES:

"What a Planner Has to Know," *Planning—1946* (Chicago: American Society of Planning Officials, 1947), 167–72.

"Reconstruction," *Task Magazine* (Editor.) Cambridge, Vol. 7, No. 8 (1948).

"Research and City Planning," *Journal of the American Institute of Planners* (Autumn 1954), 201–05.

"Shelter and Urban Renewal," *Proceedings, American Municipal Congress* (1955), 104–13.

"Will a Housing Code Protect Obsolescent Neighborhoods," *Transactions, National Safety Council,* Vol. 12 (1955), pp. 7–10.

"The University and the Apprentice," *Planning—1954* (Chicago: American Society of Planning Officials, 1956), 169–75.

"Building the Middle-Range Bridge for Comprehensive Planning," *Journal of the American Institute of Planners,* Vol. 22 (Spring 1956), 58–64.

Harvey S. Perloff

BOOKS AND PAMPHLETS:

Puerto Rico's Economic Future. Chicago: The University of Chicago Press, 1950.

(With others.) *Economic Development of Puerto Rico: 1940–1950 and 1951–1960.* San Juan: Puerto Rican Planning Board, 1951.

The University of Chicago and the Surrounding Community. Chicago: Program of Education and Research in Planning, 1953.

Urban Renewal in a Chicago Neighborhood: An Appraisal of the Hyde Park–Kenwood Renewal Program. Chicago: Hyde Park Herald, 1955.

(With Richard Meier.) *Long-Range Planning of Governmental Activities.* (In preparation.)

ARTICLES:

"Dynamic Elements in a Full Employment Program," *Income, Employment and Public Policy: Essays in Honor of A. H. Hansen* (New York: W. W. Norton, 1948), pp. 199–217.

"How Shall We Train the Planners We Need?" *Planning—1951* (Chicago: American Society of Planning Officials, 1952), 13–22.

"The United States and the Economic Development of Puerto Rico," *Journal of Economic History,* Vol. 12 (Winter 1952), 45–59.

"Requirements of an Effective Point Four Program," *Economic Development and Cultural Change,* Vol. 1 (October 1952), 209–15.

"Transforming the Economy," *Puerto Rico: A Study in Democratic Development (The Annals of the American Academy of Political and Social Science,* Vol. 285 [January 1953]), 48–54.

"Knowledge Needed for Comprehensive Planning," *Needed Urban and Metropolitan Research,* Donald J. Bogue, ed. (Oxford, Ohio: Scripps Foundation, 1953), 4–6.

"Planning Concepts and Regional Research," *Social Forces,* Vol. 32 (December 1953), 173–77.

(With A. Dollinger and G. D. N. Worswick.) "The Organization of Economic Intelligence, With Special Reference to Turkey," *United Nations Technical Report* (August 1954).

"Problems of Assessing Regional Economic Progress," *Regional Income,* Studies in Income and Wealth, Vol. 21, National Bureau of Economic Research (Princeton: Princeton University Press, 1957), 37–62.

Rexford G. Tugwell

BOOKS AND PAMPHLETS:

The Place of Planning in Society. San Juan: Puerto Rico Planning Board, 1954.

The Fourth Power and Other Approaches to Planning. (In preparation.)

The Art of Politics. (In preparation.)

ARTICLES:

"Preliminary Draft of a World Constitution," *Common Cause,* Vol. 1 (March 1948), co-author.

"The Utility of the Future in the Present," *Public Administration Review,* Vol. 8 (Winter 1948), 49–59.

"The Study of Planning as a Scientific Endeavor," *Fiftieth Annual Report of the Michigan Academy of Science, Arts, and Letters* (1948), 34–48.

"A Planner's View of Agriculture's Future," *Journal of Farm Economics*, Vol. 31 (February 1949), 29–47.

"Beyond Malthus: Numbers and Resources," *Common Cause*, Vol. 2 (May 1949), 375–77.

"Earthbound: The Problem of Planning and Survival," *Antioch Review* Vol. 9 (December 1949), 476–94.

"Letters from Latter-Day Britain," *Common Cause* (a series beginning March 1950 and continuing through June 1951, fifteen articles).

(With Edward C. Banfield.) "Grass Roots Democracy: Myth or Reality," *Public Administration Review*, Vol. 10 (Winter 1950), 47–55.

(———.) "Governmental Planning at Mid-Century," *The Journal of Politics*, Vol. 13 (1951), 133–63.

"L'Attitude réticente des Etats-Unis à l'égard de la Planification," *Revue Economique* (March 1953), 262–79.

"New York," *Great Cities of the World: Their Government, Politics, and Planning*, William A. Robson, ed. (London: George Allen and Unwin, 1955), 413–50.

INDEX

Ackerman, Edward A., *viii*, 72*n*, 106*n*
Adams, Frederick J., 9*n*, 19, 19*n*, 20*n*, 37*n*, 60, 61; on requirements for planning education, 37
Adams, Thomas, 60
Agricultural Adjustment Administration, 79*n*
Allegheny County Planning Commission, 75
Amazon area, economic development of, 106*n*
American City Planning Institute, 6, 13, 56
American Institute of Architects, 137
American Institute of Planners, 56; Committee on Planning Education, report of, 59–60
American Society of Planning Officials, 2*n*, 17*n*, 50*n*, 58, 137, 139
Anderson, William, 117*n*
Architects, role in city planning, 6, 9–11, 62
Arkansas-White-Red Basins Inter-Agency Committee, 87
Ascher, Charles S., 29*n*
ASPO. *See* American Society of Planning Officials
Augur, Tracy, *viii*
Australia, city planning in, 9*n*

Banfield, Edward C., 142*n*, 168–69, 171, 173; and Chicago Planning

Program, 139
Barfod, Børge, 114*n*
Bartholomew, Harland, 34*n*, 56
Bassett, Edward M., 13, 13*n*
Bettman, Alfred, 13, 13*n*
Blakeman, T. L., *viii*
Bloom, Benjamin, *viii*
Blucher, Walter H., 137, 140*n;* on changing approach to city planning, 17*n*
Bogue, Donald J., 71*n*–72*n*, 119*n*
Boorstin, Daniel J., 92*n*
Boston, Mass., 76; Metropolitan District Commission, 83; metropolitan park system, plan for, 54; metropolitan urban planning in, 76
Branch, Melville C., Jr., *viii*, 169; and Chicago Planning Program, 139
Brazil, valley development projects in, 106*n*
British Columbia, University of, 152
Brown University, population and human ecology seminars, 124*n*
Burdell, Edwin S., on planning in a democratic society, 34*n;* on shortage of planners, 50*n*–51*n*
Bureau of the Census, 82*n*
Bureau of Indian Affairs, 87*n*
Bureau of Land Management, 87*n*
Bureau of Mines, 87*n*